Human Rights in Global World

Human Rights in Global World

A. N. Dange

MD Publications Pvt Ltd
New Delhi
www.mdppl.com

Published by :

MD Publications Pvt Ltd
"MD House", 11, Darya Ganj,
New Delhi - 110 002
Phone : +91-11- 45355555
E-mail : contact@mdppl.com
Website: www.mdppl.com

ISBN : 978-81-7533-341-3

Published and Printed by Mr. Pranav Gupta on behalf of **MD Publications Pvt Ltd** at Repro India Limited.

Preface

Human rights are "rights and freedoms to which all humans are entitled." Proponents of the concept usually assert that everyone is endowed with certain entitlements merely by reason of being human. Human rights are thus conceived in a universalist and egalitarian fashion. Such entitlements can exist as shared norms of actual human moralities, as justified moral norms or natural rights supported by strong reasons, or as legal rights either at a national level or within international law. However, there is no consensus as to the precise nature of what in particular should or should not be regarded as a human right in any of the preceding senses, and the abstract concept of human rights has been a subject of intense philosophical debate and criticism.

A series of international human rights treaties and other instruments adopted since 1945 have conferred legal form on inherent human rights and developed the body of international human rights. Other instruments have been adopted at the regional level reflecting the particular human rights concerns of the region and providing for specific mechanisms of protection. Most States have also adopted constitutions and other laws which formally protect basic human rights. While international treaties and customary law form the backbone of international human rights law other instruments, such as declarations, guidelines and principles adopted at the international level contribute to its understanding, implementation and development. Respect for human rights requires the establishment of the rule of law at the national and international levels.

International human rights law lays down obligations which States are bound to respect. By becoming parties to international treaties, States assume obligations and duties under international law to respect, to protect and to fulfill human rights. The obligation to respect means that States must refrain from interfering with or curtailing the enjoyment of human rights. The obligation to protect requires States to protect individuals and groups against human rights abuses. The obligation to fulfill means that States must take positive action to facilitate the enjoyment of basic human rights.

The international human rights movement was strengthened when the United Nations General Assembly adopted of the Universal Declaration of Human Rights (UDHR) on 10 December 1948. Drafted as 'a common standard of achievement for all peoples and nations', the Declaration for the first time in human history spell out basic civil, political, economic, social and cultural rights that all human beings should enjoy. It has over time been widely accepted as the fundamental norms of human rights that everyone should respect and protect. The UDHR, together with the International Covenant on Civil and Political Rights and its two Optional Protocols, and the International Covenant on Economic, Social and Cultural Rights, form the so called International Bill of Human Rights.

Human Rights as a common standard of achievement for all peoples and all nations, to the end that every individual and every origin of society, keeping this Declaration constantly in mind, shall strive by teaching and education to promote respect for these rights and freedoms and by progressive measures, national and international, to secure their universal and effective recognition and observance, both among the peoples of Member States themselves and among the peoples of territories under their jurisdiction. All human beings are born free and equal in dignity and rights. They are endowed with reason and conscience and should act towards one another in a spirit of brotherhood. Human Rights is entitled to all the rights and freedoms set forth in this Declaration, without distinction of any kind, such as race, colour, sex, language, religion, political or other opinion, national or social origin, property, birth or other status. Furthermore, no distinction shall be made on the basis of the political, jurisdictional or international status of the country or territory to which a person belongs, whether it is independent, trust, non-self-governing or under any other limitation of sovereignty.

I am very grateful to Mr. Pranav Gupta, Director of MD Publications Pvt Ltd, New Delhi, for his kind cooperation and support for this book.

A. N. Dange

CONTENTS

1

Universal Declaration of Human Rights

Introduction

The creation of the Universal Declaration of Human Rights (UDHR) in 1948 marked the foundation of the modern human rights movement. It took the notion of rights and articulated it on the international level, as applicable to all. Fifty years later, the human rights movement is a truly global phenomenon, as individuals around the world cite the declaration and its rights as a way of describing their needs.

This chapter evaluates the declaration. It describes the historical context in which it was created, and then it examines the drafting process. Finally it examines the declaration itself what it stands for, what its status is, how it works, how it views human rights promotion, and how it can claim to be universal. The following chapter evaluates each of the declaration's thirty articles in turn what they mean, what the drafters' intentions were, how they have been elaborated on in subsequent instruments, and what issues they speak to today.

Historical Background of the Declaration

In many ways the declaration and the human rights movement that followed from it came out of the worldwide revulsion at the atrocities that were committed during World War II. The declaration served as a direct rebuttal of the racist and fascist ideologies that had "disregard and contempt for human rights" at their root and led to "barbarous acts which have outraged the conscience of mankind" (UDHR preamble). The "Four Freedoms," as proclaimed by President Roosevelt in his State of the Union address to Congress on January 6, 1941, were repeated in the UDHR preamble: freedom of speech and belief and freedom from fear and want. These freedoms were seen as the "highest aspirations of the common people" (UDHR preamble), and when transformed into human rights provisions, became the basis for the new world order that the Allies hoped to create after the end of the war.

The United Nations (UN) was created by the Allies (who also called themselves the "United Nations" during the war) as the cornerstone of this new world order; the organization personified the "consciousness of mankind" that had been outraged during the war. In one of several references to human rights, the UN Charter begins by proclaiming a "faith in fundamental human rights, in the dignity and worth of the human person, in the equal rights of men and women and of nations large and small" (UN Charter preamble).

The charter then charges the organization with the task of achieving "international cooperation in promoting and encouraging respect for human rights and fundamental freedoms" (Article 1), and affirms members' obligations to respect human rights in general and to work jointly and severally for their protection. Both states and nongovernmental organizations (NGOs) pushed for the inclusion of a bill of rights in the charter. However, the charter did not end up containing specific provisions on the content of human rights. Instead it was decided that this would be articulated in one of the first legislative initiatives of the organization drafting an International Bill of Rights.

Drafting the Declaration

The declaration was a product of the UN legislative process, involving various UN bodies. The Economic and Social Council (ECOSOC) mandated its subset, the eighteen-member Human Rights Commission (chaired by Eleanor Roosevelt), to draft the International Bill of Rights. Originally this was to take the form of a declaration (a statement of principles), a convention (containing the legal obligations of states), and measures of implementation (to enforce the obligations). The convention's name was changed to "covenant" and was then split into two covenants the International Covenant on Civil and Political Rights (ICCPR) and the International Covenant on Economic, Social and Cultural Rights (ICESCR) each incorporating elements of implementation within its structure.

The Human Rights Commission set up a drafting committee to formulate a draft of the declaration, based on an outline of proposals and supporting documents prepared by the Human Rights Division of the Secretariat, the permanent team of international civil servants at the UN. Input was given by the Commission on the Status of Women as well as the subcommissions (of the Human Rights Commission) on the Freedom of Information and the Press, and the Prevention of Discrimination and the Protection of Minorities. Some states also submitted suggested texts for the declaration.

The Human Rights Commission's draft was then considered by ECOSOC. The text approved by ECOSOC was then proposed as a resolution before the General Assembly, the main legislative body in the UN where every member state has an equal vote.

As chair of the drafting committee, Eleanor Roosevelt had intended that it be composed of herself and three other members of the Human Rights Commission. Under pressure from other countries, however, she was forced to expand this to include more members. This varied in number throughout the committee's existence, and members included the distinguished French legal scholar Rene Cassin, as well as representatives from Australia, China, Chile, France, the Philippines, Lebanon, USSR, the Ukranian SSR, the United Kingdom, Uruguay, and Yugoslavia.

The original outline for the declaration was prepared largely by the Canadian international lawyer John Humphrey, who worked as head of the Human Rights Division throughout the drafting process. The drafting committee then asked Rene Cassin to draft a text, using Humphrey's outline. The contents of this draft formed the basis for the eventual wording of the declaration, and for this reason Cassin has been considered as the main "author" of it. However, Humphrey's memoirs and more recent research suggest that Cassin's draft relied heavily on Humphrey's proposal. It would seem that Humphrey deserves considerable credit for the drafting of the declaration, alongside Cassin.

At the time, Humphrey claimed that there was no particular philosophical basis for the outline, stating that it was a random synthesis of proposals sent to the Secretariat from all around the world. Humphrey subsequently acknowledged that this was not actually the case. He wrote, "With two exceptions all these texts came from English-speaking sources and all of them from the democratic West. My draft attempted to combine humanitarian liberalism with social democracy. I had myself decided what to put in and what to leave out."

Humphrey and other drafters were influenced by some of the foundational constitutional documents of the United States and Europe, such as the 1215 Magna Carta (England);

the 1689 Bill of Rights (England); the 1789 Declaration of the Rights of Man (France); the 1787 United States Constitution and 1791 Bill of Rights. (These antecedents are discussed in detail in Part 1, Chapter 1.) These were complemented by specific proposals from national and international organizations and private individuals. Organizations included the United Nations Educational, Scientific, and Cultural Organization (UNESCO), the American Law Institute, the American Jewish Congress, the Women's Trade Union League, and the Inter-American Bar Association. Individuals included the author H. G. Wells, the distinguished international legal scholar Hersch Lauterpacht, and in UNESCO's report, the political scientists E. H. Carr and Harold Laski.

Although the Secretariat later cited extracts from the constitutions of a wide group of countries, this was done to foster an impression of a universal consensus in anticipation of the debates that would take place in ECOSOC and the General Assembly. Since the key decisions as to the content of the declaration were made at the drafting committee stage, inspiration for and conception of the rights in the declaration undoubtedly came primarily from the philosophical traditions and crucible of experience of the North American, European, and British Commonwealth members of the Drafting Committee and Secretariat.

The declaration was drafted during a window of opportunity after the end of World War II and before the tensions of the Cold War became so pronounced that international consensus was impossible. Even so, ideological conflict between the West and the Soviets figured in all of the debates up to and including the adoption of the declaration. Eleanor Roosevelt's shrewd tactic of making the declaration take the form of a nonbinding General Assembly resolution meant that it passed despite profound disagreements between states, since it was seen as not creating obligations for them in international law.

The covenants, on the other hand, were binding. They were not completed until 1966 and did not enter into force until 1976. Even now, many countries have not agreed to be fully bound by both the covenants, including, ironically, the United States. Similarly, the initiative for methods of implementation lost impetus because of states' reluctance to accept what they perceived as a violation of their sovereignty. Instead, elements of implementation became part of the covenants and have been introduced in a piecemeal fashion in other UN initiatives.

The effect of the Cold War on the drafting process was that two models of ideological models that followed from the Enlightenment competed to be reflected in the declaration. The Western capitalist model, with its emphasis on individualism, enterprise, and property rights, focused more on civil and political rights. The Soviet communist model, with its emphasis on group rights, individual duties, and the collective ownership of property, focused on economic, social, and cultural rights. The result was a declaration that accepted the importance of both individual liberty and the collective unit within which individuals live. Its seemingly unqualified formulation of free expression (Article 19) appealed to libertarians; the right to an adequate standard of living (Article 25) appealed to socialists.

The balance of the declaration as a whole, however, is unmistakably Western. As the driving force behind it, Eleanor Roosevelt frequently stamped down Soviet attempts to socialize it to a greater extent than was acceptable to her. (According to a *New York Times* reporter who covered the Human Rights Commission, "The Russians seem to have met their match in Mrs. Roosevelt.") For example, economic and social rights were not articulated in terms of the state's obligations to make provisions for its people where necessary (even though this is clearly the implication). Similarly the limitations that were the logical corollary to many civil and political rights (an individual is limited in exercising his or her rights if they infringe the rights of another individual, for example) were dealt with in a separate article (29) rather than as part of each right. This lays greater emphasis on rights than on the duties to the state, which were of particular importance to socialist countries.

It is worth noting that concepts of economic, social, and cultural rights were not as antithetical to the West when the declaration was drafted as they would become in the later stages of the Cold War. The social agenda of postwar reconstruction in Europe and President Roosevelt's New Deal in the United States meant that, anticommunist sentiments notwithstanding, there was significant support in the West for the state's role in promoting the economic and social welfare of its people. The socialist aspects of the declaration were, therefore, those that the West could accommodate and ran alongside civil and political rights that were passionately supported. In contrast the Soviets felt that neither the economic nor the social rights went far enough and that many of the civil and political rights were phrased in unacceptably absolutist terms.

Many of the declaration's articles were stated simply, in order to avoid taking a position on key aspects of the rights involved. To a certain degree, this was inevitable with such profound disagreements on much of the content. However, the drafters notably Eleanor Roosevelt-sincerely believed that the purpose of the declaration was to state rights in a simple fashion. It would be for subsequent instruments like the covenants to elaborate on their meaning. For example, Eleanor Roosevelt objected to the proposal that Article 20, the right to assembly, should include examples of assemblies that are permitted. She felt that this was unnecessary, and the idea was dropped.

When the declaration proposal reached the General Assembly, the third committee of that body spent considerable time in debate before the vote in the full chamber. However, Humphrey reported that despite this the "final result was remarkably like the [Human Rights] Commission's text." The General Assembly passed the resolution (217[III]A) on December 10, 1948, eighteen months after the drafting process began. There were forty-eight votes in favour, eight abstentions, and two countries absent.

Foundation of Human Rights Law

International human rights law is a body of instruments and customary norms that, although existing between states, governs the relationship between states and their peoples rather than states and other states. As such, states have agreed on the international level how they will behave on the national level. How they treat their citizens becomes a matter of international, as well as national, law.

Although international law had made some progress in the formation of human rights norms, it was at a primitive stage at the time of the drafting of the UDHR. Customary norms covered only the most basic of human rights issues (such as the prohibition on slavery) and instruments were selective in both their subject matter (e.g., the Red Cross conventions on human rights during conflict) and the states that were covered by them (e.g., the Minorities Treaties imposed on some of the defeated powers of World War I).

The declaration built on these developments and created a fully formed charter, setting out the complete range of rights applicable to all people in the world. Rather like the creation of a bill of rights on a national level, the declaration was the first time that rights had been articulated in a comprehensive manner on the international level.

In doing so, it put the human being at the center of international law. The ultimate authority for the declaration is not states, but the qualities of humanity that all the people of the world share. This is because, as the preamble states, "recognition of the inherent dignity and of the equal and inalienable rights of all members of the human family is the foundation of freedom, justice and peace in the world."

The focus away from the state to the individual is why the declaration is "universal" rather than "international."

Indeed, the declaration suggests that human rights observance is the prerequisite for state authority. The state is given respect by its citizens and by other states because it is the legitimate representative of the collective of individuals within its control. Human rights principles represent the contract between the individual and their state that is the basis for this legitimacy. Both agree to abide by rights and obligations that allow the state to protect the interests of all individuals without restricting the rights of any given individual any more than is necessary. For a state to be legitimate, therefore, it has to keep to the contract. If the state breaks it (when there is "tyranny and oppression"), it is no longer worthy of respect and has lost the authority to govern. Taking its cue from the philosopher Thomas Paine, the preamble states that "it is essential, if man is not to be compelled to have recourse, as a last resort, to rebellion against tyranny and oppression, that human rights should be protected by the rule of law." This qualified notion of legitimacy makes human rights scrutiny on the international level compatible with state sovereignty. Human rights are no longer only of concern nationally; they are a global issue.

Nature of the Declaration

An international legal instrument often consists of a preamble, which contains statements of principle, and articles, which contain substantive provisions that, if part of a treaty, are binding on states that ratify it. The declaration is not as straightforward.

As has been stated, the declaration forms part of the International Bill of Rights, together with the International Covenant on Civil and Political Rights (ICCPR) and the International Covenant on Economic, Social, and Cultural Rights (ICESCR). It was intended as a preamble style statement of principles, with the Covenants then containing substantive provisions. The declaration was passed as a nonbinding resolution of the UN General Assembly; the covenants are treaties that states ratify and are bound by. It is misleading, however, to see the declaration as merely a statement of principle. Both internally and externally, the declaration has enforceable elements to it.

Internally, the declaration makes a distinction between a preamble and articles. Many of the articles are clearly capable of being enforced, since they became the basis for the enforceable articles in the covenants and have been lifted into the text of many national constitutions. Other articles, on the other hand, are more preamble-style statements of principle that either stand alone (Article 1 on the philosophical basis of human rights; Article 28 on the conditions necessary for rights to be realized) or lead onto the more substantive rights (Article 2 on the equality that is the basis for nondiscrimination in Article 7; Article 22 on the economic, social, and cultural rights that are then set out in Articles 23-27).

Externally, the declaration has come to have considerable influence in international law, notwithstanding its status as a nonbinding General Assembly resolution that represents a "common standard of achievement" (preamble). It confirmed human rights as an integral component of international law. This in turn highlighted states' obligations in customary international law to refrain from certain practices that violated rights. In 1984 the UN Human Rights Committee stated that, according to customary international law, a State may not . . . engage in slavery, . . torture, . . subject persons to cruel, inhuman or degrading treatment or punishment, to arbitrarily deprive persons of their lives, to arbitrarily arrest and detain persons, to deny freedom of thought, conscience and religion, to presume a person guilty unless he proves his innocence, to execute pregnant women or children, to permit the advocacy of national, racial or religious hatred, to deny to persons of marriageable age the right to marry, or to deny to minorities the right to enjoy their culture, profess their religion, or use their own language . . . [and generally speaking deny] the right to a fair trial.

Therefore, although the declaration may itself fall short of being enforceable on states, many of its provisions are at the very least binding against them because of customary international law.

Concept of Human Rights

The declaration is concerned with the rights of individuals. Rights are what individuals are entitled to, by virtue of being human beings. This is therefore a focus on the most basic elements of being human. The drafters attempted to sum up the essential needs that they felt all individuals have, irrespective of differences between them, such as culture, religion, nationality, and gender.

The declaration splits these needs up into two categories civil and political rights, on the one hand, and economic and social rights on the other. The categories are sometimes called "first" and "second" generation rights respectively.

Civil and political rights are those which, broadly, concern individuals enjoying control over their own lives. The declaration covers them in Articles 2-21, and they include the principles of equal treatment (Articles 2 and 7) and freedom of expression (Article 19). They often operate in a negative sense, in that they declare the right of an individual not to be prevented from doing something (e.g., joining an association, Article 20) or not to be treated in a certain way (e.g., being held in slavery, Article 4). In order to protect negative rights, the state must refrain from interfering in the individual's life.

Economic, social, and cultural rights are those which, broadly, concern the welfare of individuals in the sense of how they can support and sustain themselves. The declaration covers them in Articles 22-27, and they include the right to work (Article 23) and the right to education (Article 26). They often operate in a positive sense, in that they declare the right of an individual to have something (e.g., a humane standard of living, Article 25). In order to protect positive rights, the state must do or give something to improve the individual's life.

However, the distinction between positive and negative rights as between civil and political rights and economic and social rights is not straightforward. Although some civil and political rights require the state in effect to do nothing (e.g., not to torture individuals, Article 5), many actually require some form of positive action. This includes enforcing the negative obligations of individuals not to restrict the rights of others (e.g., preventing private individuals from torturing other individuals) and providing procedural guarantees that safeguard the protection of rights and the rule of law (e.g., the right to a remedy for violations, Article 8). Similarly, although many economic, social, and cultural rights require the state to take positive action (e.g., providing social security, Article 22), some involve negative obligations, requiring the state not to interfere with individual choice (e.g., the right to free choice of employment, Article 23). Generally, human rights law scrutinizes a state's adherence to negative rights differently from its promotion of positive rights, since the former does not depend on the level of resources available to the state in the same way that the latter does.

In seeking to guarantee the realization of individuals' needs, human rights are necessarily concerned with regulating the relationship between individuals and those who affect this realization. Just as international law has traditionally concerned states, so international human rights law although introducing the individual as a subject of international law is conventionally seen as concerning the rights of individuals as against the state (the "public" actor), rather than as against other individuals or entities ("private" actors). Therefore, the right to education, for example, is about the state ensuring that individuals within its country are provided with education.

The enjoyment of some rights is influenced almost solely by the state, such as the right to a nationality (Article 15). However, the enjoyment of many rights is often influenced by both public and private actors. The right to education, for example, is affected by the state (e.g., in its operation of state-run schools) and by private actors (e.g., parents making choices for their children; the operation of privately run schools). Human rights law regulates both actors via the state: the public actor directly and the private actor indirectly. This is because the state, as the sovereign authority, can be construed as having ultimate responsibility not only for its own actions but also for the actions of those within its jurisdiction. For example, if a private school provides education in a discriminatory manner (contrary to Articles 7 and 26) and the state does nothing about it, then the state is arguably liable in international human rights law.

Recently this distinction between public and private has been criticized by those who argue that human rights law should be brought to bear on the behaviour of private actors in a more imaginative way. Feminists argue, for example, that the starting point of public liability inevitably makes human rights focus more on those abuses perpetrated against men (e.g., when dealt with by the police, a public body) than those perpetrated against women (e.g., domestic violence, which takes place in a private place and involves a private actor). More generally, in a globalized and fragmented world, private actors from multinational corporations to militias are in many respects as determinative of individuals' rights as states. This shifts the balance away from the state's direct liability for its own actions to its indirect liability for the actions of those within its jurisdiction.

The drafters clearly had in mind the obligations of the state when they created the declaration. However, they drafted it in a way that deliberately left open the scope for conceiving ways of promoting rights and did not limit their focus to the behaviour of states. Fifty years after the declaration, human rights scholars are beginning to suggest ways in which private actors can be brought within the purview of human rights law in a more meaningful way.

Human rights regulates relationships to enable individuals to realize their needs in different ways. Often such relationships involve rights and responsibilities (or duties) on both sides. For example, the right to freedom of religion (Article 18) concerns the individual's right to practice his or her religion but his or her duty not to force it on other people (which would violate other individuals' rights to practice their religions). This corresponds to the state's duty not to restrict the individual's practice of his or her religion in normal circumstances, but its right to do so when this involves forcing religious beliefs on other people. Sometimes, however, individual rights are absolute (such as the right not to be tortured in Article 5), in that the state has no right to restrict them in any circumstances.

The declaration articulates a model for regulating relationships which places an emphasis first and foremost on the individual's rights. In doing so it presumes that an individual is entitled to a right and requires a state to justify limiting the right if this is possible. In its practical application, therefore, human rights often amount to an evaluation of the legitimate boundaries of the state. The principles of Article 29, which test whether a state's limitation on rights is justified, are central to many human rights questions.

The declaration is a "common standard of achievement for all peoples and all nations" (preamble). It is a set of fundamental principles that applies to all people because it is rooted in the universal needs of the human condition. It tests particular situations to evaluate what an individual's entitlements are. In doing so, it takes into account the context in which the situation takes place. For example, with the right to education the amount of provision necessary depends on the resources of a state. A developed country would be expected to make more education available than a developing country. The "common standard" is whether both are making the best effort they can to direct all available resources to areas outlined in human rights law.

Declaration Envisions the Promotion of Human Rights

The declaration began what has become a worldwide movement to promote "universal respect for and observance of human rights" (preamble). This involves evaluating the human rights situation in countries to see whether it complies with international human rights law.

The drafters saw the promotion of human rights as important to develop "friendly relations between nations" (preamble). They had in mind the risk to peace posed by states who did not safeguard rights in their own territories and wished to enforce concepts that violated rights (e.g., the superiority of a certain race) on other countries through violent means. The promotion of human rights in other states has now become a key part of the foreign policy of many countries, such as the United States. If respect for a state's sovereignty depends on the level of human rights protection in that country, then indirect and even direct interference from outside becomes justifiable. Thus human rights promotion by states can actually lead to hostile relations between nations-but from an attempt to promote rights, not destroy them.

The declaration envisions a broad range of enforcement mechanisms that reflect the diverse nature of human rights issues. It proclaims the necessity of "progressive measures, national and international" to ensure the "universal and effective recognition and observance" of rights (Preamble).

The UN plays a key role in this process, by setting human rights standards and then monitoring states' compliance. States, NGOs, and international organizations have all been involved in implementing measures to promote human rights. These have ranged from coordinating development strategies (e.g., the activities of the UN Development Program) to sanctions (e.g., against apartheid-era South Africa).

The declaration insists, however, that this "recognition and observance" of human rights has to be "universal and effective" (preamble). It is not enough that states sign up to human rights treaties, if they continue to violate rights within their country. It is not enough for states to appraise other countries according to the standards of human rights, if they are not prepared to accept such standards themselves. It is not enough that some states observe human rights standards, if other states do not. It is not enough for human rights promotion mechanisms to deal with rights issues on a particular scale (e.g., individual violations) if they cannot deal effectively with those on another scale (e.g., mass violations of human rights like "disappearances").

Human rights promotion does not merely involve the creation of legal provisions on a national and international level. The principles that these laws uphold should become part of cultures and societies generally. People should be aware of their rights, and the language of rights should inform the way they relate to each other, their communities, and their country. The drafters had this in mind when they stated in the preamble that "every individual and every organ of society shall strive by teaching and education to promote respect for these rights and freedoms." This in turn should lead states and other actors who play a decisive role in the lives of individuals to evaluate the boundaries of this role in terms of human rights principles. Therefore, it is important that the process of raising awareness is seen as a goal in its own right, rather than a spin-off of human rights law enforcement.

Declaration Can Claim to Be Universal

For an instrument that proclaims itself universal, the declaration came out of a process that was far from globally inclusive. It was based on the philosophical traditions of the West and drafted by a handful of individuals mostly from the West. It was passed in a General Assembly where many countries in the world were not represented because they were colonies (only one African country-Egypt was a member), through a vote in which socialist countries abstained.

For this reason, the declaration and the human rights movement that it precipitated have been criticized as a neo-imperialist attempt by the West to "civilize" the majority of the world's peoples who do not share their cultural heritage. Indeed, the entire structure of international law is based on European notions of state sovereignty. The countries that emerged from colonialism or had been powerless during the so-called "Age of Empire" had little choice but to accept a system that they played no direct part in creating.

However, the power of the declaration is precisely that it has transcended the circumstances in which it was drafted. It has been able to do so because of two important features: its emphasis on the indivisibility of all rights and its simple enunciation of them.

First, the combined effect of Cold War compromise and New Deal social democracy created a declaration that forcefully underlined what has become a fundamental principle of human rights: the indivisibility of civil and political rights on the one hand, and economic and social rights on the other. The preamble reminds states that in the UN Charter they "reaffirmed their faith in fundamental human rights, in the dignity and worth of the human person and in the equal rights of men and women and have determined to promote social progress and better standards of life in larger freedom."

In articulating a model of interdependent civil, political, economic, social, and cultural rights, the declaration makes a bold attempt to incorporate all of the various needs that are emphasized differently around the world. Whereas some in the developed world view rights mainly in civil and political terms, this is a misrepresentation of the declaration. To object to a nation's emphasis on civil and political rights is not to object to the declaration itself, merely to a selective view of it.

Second, in phrasing rights in simple terms, the declaration managed, mostly, to sum up the basic human needs that prevail regardless of considerable changes in circumstances. The human rights instruments that came after it were necessary to flesh out the rights and explain how they could be realized in a practical manner. Inevitably, however, this makes them more contingent on the particular circumstances of the time when they were drafted and the views of those who drafted them. The European Commission on Human Rights, for example, included an exception to the right to life allowing judicial execution, a practice that was carried out in several European states at the time. Now it has been abolished in all the original states of the Council of Europe, and new member states are required to sign a protocol outlawing the death penalty.

The declaration, in contrast, has managed to retain meaningfulness despite the profound changes in history, politics, culture, and development since the time of its drafting. Peoples struggling for independence from colonial rule used it as the inspiration for their claim to self-determination. Groups in the West, such as the lesbian, gay, and bisexual community, invoke the principles of the declaration to support their rights in ways that would have been inconceivable when it was drafted but which are nevertheless consistent with its provisions. The nations of Africa, when drafting the African Charter on Human and People's Rights, emphasized individual duties as well as rights and so elaborated on the provisions of Article 29.

The declaration, therefore, stands as a beacon for the potential of the human rights movement, rather than a fixed code that has no relevance in these postmodern times. Despite the lack of progress in the international protection of human rights during the Cold War (the UDHR was the only global human rights instrument from 1948 to 1976) the declaration reemerged in the 1990s as the core of a new human rights movement. This movement is not about Western governments seeking to export their version of democracy, either as an alternative to Communism or to redeem the people of the developing world. It is not about "us" who have rights, and "them" who don't.

The contemporary human rights movement is a genuinely global phenomenon, as individuals around the world use the declaration as the starting point for articulating the needs that they have. A very different General Assembly from that which passed the declaration, this time made up of countries from all around the world, continues to elaborate many of the principles within the declaration. This has created a human rights agenda that is both rooted in the declaration and genuinely reflective of the diversity of needs around the world.

The language of human rights has been reclaimed from states and their leaders by the very people to whom the declaration originally spoke. States that have traditionally seen human rights as something to be exported, like the United States and United Kingdom, now find their own human rights records being criticized by the very movement they helped to create. Authoritarian leaders who claim that human rights are incompatible with their peoples' cultures find those very people using the language of rights against them.

In both cases, value is added to the validity of human rights as a genuinely universal phenomenon. It is "brought home" to those countries that are complacent; it is refashioned to reflect the human rights struggles of different cultures and regions.

Eleanor Roosevelt intended that the declaration be a "living instrument" so that it could precipitate the "common understanding" of rights and freedoms that the preamble states "is of the greatest importance." This approach can be credited for the continuing relevance and utility of the declaration to the human rights issues that people face. It is an inspiration for each individual's articulation of his or her particular needs; as Eleanor Roosevelt said, an "international magna carta for all men everywhere."

2

Politics of Human Rights

Introduction

Human rights discourse has become irrepressible all over the world and few states would publicly justify their denial of a democratic form of government. Nevertheless it is doubtful that the Human Rights Commission and the General Assembly of today would underwrite the Universal Declaration as it was proclaimed in 1948. The opposition would not only come from authoritarian governments. Several Western countries would be reluctant to support the social and economic rights defined in the Declaration, in particular the right to work or protection against unemployment. Conservative ideology is so dominant today that many states have become hesitant to protect obligations that might hamper free exchange of goods and services or alter the sacrosanct principles of competition and productivity. Moreover globalization tends to erode state sovereignty and governments' capacity to deliver the public goods which are necessary for the implementation of human rights. Before tackling this last issue, I intend to clarify some common misunderstandings about the universality of human rights.

Historical Background

The debate on universality bears a clear resemblance to the discussion on natural law. Are there some abstract norms to which any rational individual could adhere to all over the world? Philosophers and anthropologists have been struggling with this issue for ages and I doubt whether the recurrent dispute within the United Nations adds anything new to this debate. Although some common norms might exist in every society, such as the prohibition of incest and of killing, human rights cannot be universal unless they are understood to comprise a very limited definition of human dignity. Human rights should not be conceived as abstract principles and ideals of individual liberty and justice. They entail by definition a system of rights and obligations which necessitates a political order founded on democratic institutions and social welfare. Effective universality would require a world society ruled by a common government capable of implementing human rights as a set of positive laws to be valid everywhere. Fortunately there is nothing of this sort and therefore states will continue to hold ultimate responsibility for the promotion and defence of human rights. They will necessarily have their own institutions, legal arrangements, and social policies for the protection of these norms.

The intellectual origins of human rights are diverse and complex. They can be traced back to all values, norms, and institutions which tend to protect human dignity and which are therefore inherent in most civilizations. However, human rights have a political, institutional, and socioeconomic history and should not be confused with a catalogue of moral values or ethical ideals uprooted from the conditions of their emergence and development. They have their origin in the humanism of the European Renaissance. It expanded as a philosophical conception of man and society during the eighteenth-century Enlightenment. In other words, it sprang from the circumstances which contributed to the development of the capitalist market and the nation state, in particular scientific and technological progress, the process of urbanization and secularization, growing individualism and egalitarianism.

Contemporary human rights, as defined in the Universal Declaration, arose from World War II and resistance to totalitarian regimes of fascist or communist inspiration. The concept first emerged within the United Nations as a set of guiding principles and norms defining the nature of political legitimacy and social welfare. It was indeed proclaimed by the General Assembly as the "common standard of achievement for all peoples and all nations." It expressed a liberal Weltanschaung on man and society. It provided a coherent doctrinal framework for a model of society reflecting the pre-eminence of the individual, but this conception was enriched by a new conception of citizenship based on the ideas of distributive justice and social protection. The Declaration recognizes that the full realization of individual rights requires specific socio-economic conditions. As a matter of fact the protection of the most basic individual rights necessitates an adequate standard of living and access to basic essentials for sustaining human existence, such as food, shelter, clothing, health care. The Declaration asserts not only a democratic, institutional and juridical model protecting individual liberty and freedom; it also proposes a policy framework. Articles 22 to 27 of the Declaration define a comprehensive set of socio-economic and cultural rights. Article 22 states, for example, that: "Everyone, as a member of society, has the right to social security and is entitled to realization, through national effort and international cooperation and in accordance with the organization and resources of each State, of the economic, social and cultural rights indispensable for his dignity and the free development of his personality."

In the perspective of the Declaration, the state must

provide the right to work, to free choice of employment, and protection against unemployment. For everyone who works, it must implement "the right to just and favourable remuneration ensuring for himself and his family an existence worthy of human dignity." It must also make sure that everyone has the right to rest and leisure and provide all the necessary components for their personal fulfilment and well-being. Education is also an essential part of human rights. The Declaration therefore gives not only content and finality to the rule of law, which is the bedrock of democracy, but it also provides a precise outline of the aims of the welfare state. As a matter of fact, this universalism expresses the dominant social democratic ideology of Western nations after World War II. It can indeed be interpreted as an attempt to give universal validity to the ideal of the welfare state.

There is no blueprint for establishing the institutional and socio-economic conditions necessary for the full realization of human rights, but unquestionably states remain the ultimate guardians of the security and welfare of individuals. States are indeed the principal authorities for political and social integration and no other source of authority actually exists to arbitrate or mitigate their internal conflicts, control market dynamics, carry out redistribution of wealth by means of tax systems, ensure protection of vulnerable groups, establish and maintain the appropriate infrastructures for production, exchange and the distribution of goods and services, as well as prevent environmental damage. The rule of law protected by democratic institutions and a fair and efficient judicial system is a prerequisite for the protection of human rights. But so is economic and social welfare whose realization depends as much on governments' public policies and socio-economic development as on legal instruments. States should not only protect civil and political rights, but also ensure fair distributive justice among social groups, granting special attention to the most vulnerable individuals and to sociological minorities. They are also responsible for developing social infrastructures such as education, vocational training, health and social security. They must create the material conditions such as transport and communication which promote economic and social well-being without degrading the environment. It has been admitted that states violate their core obligation under the Covenant on Economic, Social and Cultural Rights when a significant number of their individuals are deprived of essential foodstuffs, essential primary health care, basic shelter and housing, or the most elementary forms of education. One can agree with Jack Donnelly when he writes: "All actual liberal democratic welfare states fall short of realising all human rights even for their own nationals. Nonetheless, only such states are systematically committed to the full range of internationally recognised human rights. Only in such states do robust markets and democracies operate within systematic limits set by human rights."

Human Rights Discourses

Within the United Nations, human rights has always consisted of different overlapping discourses and concomitant practices. The first discourse is essentially ideological and defines principles of political legitimacy. The second expresses juridical norms. The third is of a political nature and includes deliberation on the strategies for implementation of human rights. I will try first to analyse the evolution of these different aspects of human rights, focusing on the major contemporary challenges of human rights implementation.

Human Rights as an Ideology

The catalogue of human rights as defined by the Universal Declaration and international covenants being very extensive, governments tend to promote a specific national discourse on these rights which reinforce their own political interests. In the 1960s, for example, third world and socialist governments used human rights, especially people's rights, as a propaganda tool to legitimize their state power and development objectives. This practice has not disappeared with the disintegration of the Soviet Empire. Several Asian governments have tried to restrict the universality of fundamental human rights by insisting on specific communitarian values which are supposed to be part of their civilization and traditions. This discourse, which came to the fore during the Vienna Conference in 1993, has sometimes been a propaganda tool to legitimize authoritarian and corrupt regimes.

On the other hand, human rights are often viewed by Western governments and public opinions as a set of principles and ideals mostly related to civil and political liberties. They envisage these norms as a decalogue of moral injunctions or ethical principles related to justice and liberty instead of reflecting on their legal, institutional, and political dimensions. In particular there is a lack of interest in the institutional mechanisms, which are necessary for their protection, such as legislative and juridical procedures. Issues related to the socio-economic conditions that facilitate their implementation are often ignored. During the Cold War, the American government used human rights as a propaganda instrument in world affairs. In so doing it promoted a conception of liberty restricted to the most basic individual, political, and civil freedom and was even selective in the promotion of these norms. The Carter administration, for example, which made civil and political rights a factor in its relations with Latin American countries, was selective since it did not aim at offending governments in Asia, Africa, or the Middle East, which were often responsible for significant or sometimes mass violations of these rights. While refraining from ratifying some fundamental human rights treaties, the United States has continued to promote a very ideological view of human rights. As Reed Broody wrote recently: "The US does not actually argue that the international bill of human rights is not of universal relevance. Rather, and more perniciously, it just consistently behaves as if human rights law does not apply to the United States." As an illustration of this bad record, Broody reminds us that, "the United States is the only country in the world, apart from Somalia, that has not ratified the Convention on the Rights of the Child. It is one of the few countries that has not ratified the Convention on the Elimination of All Forms of Discrimination against Women. It has also refused to ratify the Covenant on Economic, Social and Cultural Rights or the American Convention on Human Rights." President Clinton's last State of the Union address reminded the Congress that more than 40 million Americans are without health insurance. This also means that their life expectancy is shorter. According to the Center on Budget and Policy Priorities, 1 per cent of the American population has as much income at its disposal, after tax, in 1999 as the 100 million Americans in the lowest income bracket which make up 38 per cent of the population. This social gap has more than doubled since 1977. Although economic growth led recently to a significant reduction in poverty, the poverty rate for children is still at nearly 20 per cent, higher than in most Western industrialized countries.

In the meantime, the US government, as well as most private foundations and corporate donors, are ready to finance human rights programmes in Africa, Asia, or Latin America, but they still refuse to give a penny to monitor torture or degrading treatment of US prison inmates. According to the New York-based Organization Human Rights Watch there are currently more than 20,000 prisoners in the United States, housed in special super-maximum security units who live in inhuman conditions. They spend "their waking and sleeping hours locked in small, sometimes windowless, cells sealed with solid steel doors." They are subjected to all kinds of pointless suffering and humiliation. They often stay in these prisons for an indefinite period that may continue for years. Some inmates develop clinical symptoms associated with psychosis. For the political establishment as well as public opinion, human rights violations are supposed to happen outside the United States.

In a similar perspective, French governments, especially under President Mitterrand, have often used human rights rhetoric or humanitarian principles as an instrument for enhancing their foreign policy objectives, while promoting interests and strategies in Africa which are far from congenial to the respect of these norms. As a matter of fact, most OECD countries have increasingly blurred human rights with humanitarian ideals, the defence of the free market and abstract appeals in favour of the defence of good governance, while steadily reducing their economic assistance to developing countries, which is necessary for the promotion and implementation of these rights. NGOs active in the field of human rights have contributed to this vision. Generally from the Western world, they have committed themselves to the realization of specific individual rights, in particular freedom of opinion and expression, the prohibition of torture or slavery, but they have often failed to address the root cause of the violation of these rights and abstained from actively participating in the realization of economic, social, and cultural rights. Of course they are not unconcerned by the fact that every year more than 20 million people die of hunger, that some 800 million people suffer from chronic hunger, but they tend to consider this phenomenon as an issue which is solely development-related.

Human Rights as Law

The Universal Declaration of Human Rights was not intended to impose legal obligations, but since its adoption by the General Assembly in 1948, most states have endorsed its main provision as jus cogens. The development of legal instruments and procedural mechanisms inspired by the Universal Declaration has been particularly significant in the last decades. The United Nations has promulgated different human rights treaties which are in force. Among these the Covenant on Civil and Political Rights, the Covenant on Economic, Social and Cultural Rights, the Convention on the Elimination of All Forms of Discrimination against Women, the Convention against Torture and Other Cruel, Inhuman or Degrading Treatment or Punishment and the Convention on the Suppression and Punishment of the Crime of Apartheid. The two covenants protecting civil and political rights, as well as economic, social, and cultural rights which came into force in 1976 have in particular given stronger legal force and precision to the principle and norms of the Universal Declaration. Some 150 states have adhered to these two covenants. The Convention on the Rights of the Child was adopted by the General Assembly in its Resolution 44/25 of 20 November 1989, and came into force on 2 September 1992. Nearly every state, with the exception of Somalia and the United States has ratified it. Within the International Labour Organisation (ILO) several conventions protecting social rights have also been enacted, dealing in particular with freedom of association and collective bargaining, abolition of forced labour, equal remuneration and non-discrimination in employment. For example the questions of child labour, dangerous work, or forced labour have been addressed by a series of conventions within the framework of the ILO. Human rights are also protected at the regional level, the most sophisticated mechanisms in this respect being founded on the European Convention on Human Rights, the European Convention against Torture and the American Convention on Human Rights.

A complex institutional structure consisting of a network of bodies, organs, and complaint procedures has been developed within the United Nations as well as regional organizations to monitor and enforce these rights. On the whole the supervisory mechanisms have been weak at the international level, except within Europe. Most of them are of a nonjudicial character. UN organs and bodies receive and comment on periodic reports from state parties on the general human rights situation of their country or on more specific issues such as torture, violence against women, or the protection of children. The aim of the reporting procedure is to help governments bring their laws and practice into conformity with their treaty obligations. Unfortunately, states usually do not submit their reports on time and most of these reports aim at throwing a rosy light on their national reality. This nevertheless gives NGOs an opportunity to react and provide additional critical information. These organs or bodies issue reports, recommendations, and opinions that are legally non-binding. Some of them can also carry out fact-finding missions. The Human Rights Committee was empowered in an Optional Protocol of the Covenant on Civil and Political Rights to receive and consider complaints from individuals alleging violation of the convention by states which had accepted the right of petition, but this complaint procedure has not been widely accepted. Unfortunately, the supervisory mechanism of the Committee on the Rights of the Child does not provide for the possibility of individual communications.

The creation of an International Criminal Court, decided on 17 July 1998, by the diplomatic conference convened in Rome under the aegis of the UN is probably a major breakthrough in the promotion and protection of human rights. The idea of international responsibility of individuals is certainly not a new one, as it was accepted during World War II and implemented at the Nuremberg and Tokyo trials. However, more recent history has highlighted the importance of fighting impunity at the international level. The International Criminal Court, which is due to become operational as soon as 60 states have ratified its convention, is therefore a significant step forward in international protection of human rights and humanitarian law. The court will be capacitated to judge perpetrators of genocide, crimes against humanity, war crimes, and aggression. It will take on this responsibility each time the courts of law of any state are unable to carry out their duties. The International Court will therefore obstruct the law of impunity. This juridical procedure will not only be activated by states and the Security Council, but also by the prosecutor of the future court who will act on his or her own authority.

Nevertheless, numerous obstacles of a political nature are bound to interfere with the implementation of this mechanism. It has been admitted, thanks to the pressure of the French and US governments, that states could ratify the convention while reserving the rights of their nationals not to be prosecuted by the tribunal during the first seven years of the treaty. In addition, this reserve can be extended for another seven years. More generally, the prosecutor will probably hesitate before prosecuting for the most "common" crimes that are almost standard in many states. Nationals of powerful states or countries enjoying strong external protection will obviously be in a better position to avoid prosecution, especially if the United States refuses to support the setting-up of this new court. In any case, it is not even certain whether the United Nations will demonstrate its political will or mobilize the means necessary to prosecute for the crimes listed in the court's statutes, above all if the process of restoring order has implied long and painstaking negotiations between the protagonists.

There is a wide gap between legal obligations and state practice and the ratification of legal instruments and procedure does not always indicate the willingness or capacity of governments to respect their obligations. There are many states that ratify all possible human rights instruments without having the slightest intention or capacity to implement them. In many developing countries there is an enormous rift between the legal and institutional world and practical day-to-day political and social reality. The number of ratifications of international treaties in the field of human rights is therefore not a good indication of real progress in the protection of human dignity. In addition, more and more states have become incapable of implementing their obligations here. A chronic problem has arisen as states neglect their obligation to send in their reports or they accumulate delays in providing them. In many countries governments claim, rightly or wrongly, that they are not in control of paramilitary groups responsible for torture and disappearances. On top of this they appear unable to subdue liberation movements, terrorist groups, or Mafia-type organizations which kidnap, torture, and kill. Civil disorders of this type which have plagued countries like Colombia for decades have become extremely widespread in the 1990s. Moreover, weak states cannot control the activities of transnational corporations, which are sometimes directly responsible for widespread violation of social, economic, and cultural rights. Consequently, progress in the realization of human rights depends less on the growing number of states ratifying conventions to protect these rights than on the crucial political choices to be made at national and international levels to guarantee the conditions necessary for individual security and social well-being.

Human Rights as Politics

As a set of norms formally accepted by most states, they can signal the foundations of political order and good socio-economic policies. There has been an impressive increase in the number of NGOs and grass-roots movements which draw their legitimacy and inspiration world-wide from these international obligations. Thanks to the United Nations, human rights have become part of the political process of most countries and can also inspire a wide variety of political movements and NGOs all over the world. The UN Conference on Human Rights in 1993 admitted for example that international laws and mechanisms, which had been established to promote and protect human rights, had not so far responded adequately to the concerns of women. The Declaration and Programme of Action adopted in Vienna therefore gave a new visibility to the issue of women. In December 1993, the UN General Assembly adopted the Declaration on the Elimination of Violence against Women. Some months later the Commission on Human Rights appointed a Special Rapporteur on violence against women, its causes and consequences. On 12 March 1999, the Commission on the Status of Women adopted an Optional Protocol to the Women's Convention of 1979 which will strengthen the possibility of using this instrument to end discrimination, including violence, against women.

Paraphrasing Clemenceau, one could say that human rights are such an important issue that they cannot be left to jurists and lawyers alone. Human rights are also a policy issue and William F. Felice has rightly stressed that "we must move beyond human rights law and legal positivism to the realm of international political economy." The legal approach considers human realities without taking into account politics and social organization. This perspective can have dubious consequences. The issue of child labour is a good case in point. From a legal point of view, it is legitimate to apply the international standards of several ILO conventions that prohibit work under the age of 18. But for many children the choice does not lie simply between remunerated economic activity and education, but between work in the in formal sector, without any protection, or even prostitution and crimes. Just as development thinking was considered for too long the exclusive domain of financial institutions and economists, human rights has tended to remain the preserve of legal experts or of NGO militants and diplomats gravitating around Geneva-based UN bodies. These people are often illversed and not particularly interested in the definition of the strategies that are necessary to establish the conditions required for the protection and development of human dignity. The sectorialization of the UN system along functionalist lines has also hindered reflection on the broader aspects of human rights implementation.

In spite of this dominant legal bias, one of the most contentious issues within the United Nations has been the debate concerning the respective importance of civil and political rights versus socio-economic and cultural rights. The protection of human dignity obviously requires certain basic socio-economic conditions. The United Nations has constantly stressed the indivisibility and interdependence of these rights. This was of course reiterated in the context of the deliberations on the "right to development." The World Conference on Human Rights in 1993 reaffirmed the right to development as a universal and inalienable right and an integral part of fundamental human rights. It stated that while development facilitates the enjoyment of all human rights, the lack of development may not be invoked to justify the curtailment of internationally recognized human rights. The Human Rights Commission has recently underlined that "extreme poverty and exclusion from society constitute a violation of human dignity and that urgent national and international action is therefore required to eliminate them." It has requested states to foster participation by the poorest people in the decision-making process in the societies in which they live. It has admitted that the "existence of widespread absolute poverty inhibits the full and effective enjoyment of human rights and renders democracy and popular participation fragile." There is no freedom of expression and democracy without instruction. It is also true that the implementation of civil and political rights, such as the rights to political participation, freedom of expression and of assembly are also necessary to overcome misery and exclusion since their realization is an essential contribution to the prevention of misrule and injustice which hamper or even prevent socio-economic development. Developing countries are usually unable to provide the economic and social infrastructures that are necessary for the protection of democracy. Experts from the UN Sub-Commission on the Promotion and Protection of Human Rights have also adopted three resolutions in 2001 calling into question the impact of key aspects of the globalization process on human rights. Reacting to claims made by the IMF during the discussion that it is not bound by international human rights standards, the Sub-Commission, in a resolution on Globalization and its Impact on the Full Enjoyment of All Human Rights, reaffirmed the importance and relevance of human rights in international trade, investment, and finance. It urged all governments and international economic policy forums, including WTO, to take human rights fully into account. The Sub-Commission also expressed concern about the human rights implications of liberalization of international trade in agricultural products, especially on the right to food for members of vulnerable communities. In a second resolution applying a human rights perspective to the WTO's General Agreement on Trade in Services (GATS) for the first time, the Sub-Commission called for a report on this matter from the High Commissioner for Human Rights. It also recommended that the WTO include consideration of the human rights implications of the GATS on the provision of basic services, such as affordable and accessible health and education services. The Sub-Commission also addressed the negative impact of the WTO's Agreement on Trade-Related Aspects of Intellectual Property Rights (TRIPS) on human rights. It signalled continuing concern that the scope and meaning of several provisions of the TRIPS Agreement need to be clarified in order to ensure that states' obligations under this agreement do not contradict their binding human rights obligations. The protection of indigenous peoples' traditional knowledge, food security, access to medicine, technology transfer and development and preventing "biopiracy" are but some of the crucial human rights issues raised by the implementation of the WTO TRIPS Agreement.

Although representatives of Western governments are still reluctant to define as rights those obligations of a political or moral nature whose holders are difficult to identify, there is less disagreement nowadays within the United Nations on the definition of these norms than on the strategy to follow in order to implement them. This question cannot be resolved on an abstract normative level. It is a sensitive and conflictual problem involving the very essence of politics. It is one thing to proclaim that the right to work or the right to development should be considered as universal human rights, it is quite another to define and realize concretely the policy which will ensure the implementation of these norms.

The Contentious Impact of Globalization

It is in the context of this reflection on human rights as politics that one should examine the impact of globalization on the implementation of these norms. The acceleration of globalization in the 1980s coincided with an extensive process of democratization in Latin America. It has most probably contributed to the disintegration of the Soviet Empire. Trade liberalization, the expansion of direct foreign investment, and the rapidly changing production system have encouraged economic growth and per capita income in many parts of the developing world, especially in East Asia and Latin America.

However, the notion of globalization has turned out to be partly illusory, since the yawning socio-economic gap between different regions of the world prevails, just as it does within developing countries, although the geography of these rifts has changed in the last decades. The majority of the world population still lives off subsistence economy and hardly benefits from the distribution of goods, services, capital, and technology. Globalization has broadened the gulf between those who can integrate into the world market and those who have to stay on the sidelines of modern production and exchange systems. It has been associated within many developing countries with the worsening social conditions of the poor whose income, health, and housing are deteriorating. In its 1997 Report on World Trade and Development, UNCTAD stressed that globalization goes hand in hand with increasing inequalities between North and South. The report affirmed that: "In almost every country which has liberalised its trade, salary inequality has increased, most often in a context of a shrinkage of work on offer for low-qualified workers with ensuing drops in their wages, sometimes plummeting 20 to 30 per cent in some Latin American countries."

Economic growth is increasingly linked to improvement of productivity, but the flow of private investment to poor countries is irregular, sparse, and very selective. Investors demand preconditions economic, social, cultural, and political which are, by definition, sorely lacking in these countries. Most poor countries, especially sub-Saharan African countries, with no industry, no producers for their raw materials, which are less in demand now, abandoned by investors and traders, faced with low-output agriculture, environmental damage, an upsurge of lethal epidemics and a very high birthrate cannot escape from an economic and social slump. Globalization has also facilitated erratic movements of capital which bear no relation to production or trade. The deregulation of financial markets, which are dominated by a small number of private institutions, has increased the vulnerability of developing countries to speculative movements of short-term capital. Monetary and financial crises in Mexico, or more recently in the new industrial countries of Asia and Latin America, have engendered social crises of great magnitude, condemning millions of people to lower living standards and misery. According to UN estimates the proportion of poor people in Indonesia has risen from 11 per cent in 1997 to 40 per cent of the population today, affecting tens of millions. Korea, Thailand, and Malaysia have also been badly hit by the crisis, which has had a negative social backlash in many other emerging countries. UNDP affirms that nearly 1.3 billion people have no access to drinking water and "live" on one dollar a day: 840 million people suffer from malnutrition and the gulf between rich and poor is on the increase. The World Bank provides comparable figures with an estimate of 3 billion people living on less than two dollars a day.

As we have seen, the promotion of universal human rights requires the establishment of political conditions which favour a fair distribution of growth among social groups and the full realization of socio-economic rights at the national as well as the international level. Increasing disparities in the distribution of income both within and between societies places stress and poses an important challenge to the whole human rights system. The violence faced by street children, trafficking in women, as well as abuses by the state, or with the acquiescence of the state, against minorities are examples of these realities. Globalization has weakened state capacity to maintain the type of socio-economic regulation and distributive justice that are necessary for the full realization of human rights. It tends to undermine national specificities regarding social welfare, protection of the environment, and cultural identity. The enormous expansion of transnational corporations, coupled with the liberalization of goods and services and the deregulation of financial markets, has coincided nearly everywhere with new social polarization. States compete to attract foreign investments and this means fiscal restraints and austerity measures in order to defend the value of their currency and to balance their budget. This policy erodes states' welfare function and limits their capacity to help vulnerable people. The increasingly disturbing phenomenon of social exclusion characterized by the growing number of homeless, jobless youngsters and long-term unemployed and people living in extreme poverty on the outskirts of big cities has accompanied the upsurge of globalization within OECD countries. This process has several other negative consequences such as the increase in the number of prison inmates, especially in the United States.

Matters are made worse for poor countries by the fact that most of their social security systems are fragile, basic, or quasi non-existent. Poverty considerably hinders the state's capacity to deliver public goods that create the conditions for the realization of human rights. Adam Przeworski has confirmed empirically what intuitively appears self-evident: that there is a strong positive correlation between economic development and democracy. James Wolfensohn, President of the World Bank Group, has recently strongly emphasized good governance as a way to promote development. "A country must have an educated and well organised government. This requires capacity building, an open legislative and transparent regulatory system, properly trained and remunerated officials and an absolute commitment to clean government... Without the protection of human and property rights, and a comprehensive framework of laws, no equitable government is possible." In the 1990s, the Inter-American Development Bank also put a great deal of emphasis on judicial and institutional reform as a way to economic and social progress. It is true that many Sub-Saharan African, Central or Southern Asian states have generally continued to rely on centralized and highly personalized forms of government which are corrupt and show little respect for fundamental human rights. Unfortunately, there is also a strong positive correlation between corruption, lack of judicial independence, inaccessibility of the courts, unsatisfactory separation of powers, lack of transparency, and accountability of official institutions and poverty. The area governed by tyrannical regimes with methods which include systematic torture and forced disappearances, corresponds broadly to the world's poorest regions, where any efforts to construct a state fail dismally or turn out to be plagued with enormous obstacles.

One should recognize that democratic countries contribute little to the world-wide alleviation of poverty and therefore to the promotion of human rights on a universal basis. Most of them do not really care about the consequences of trade or financial policy for poor countries. Moreover the weakening of the welfare state in OECD countries has also coincided with the erosion of development policies concerning poor regions of the world as well as with the return to charity-related activities. Rich countries are counting on direct foreign investments and trade liberalization to promote economic growth everywhere. They therefore tend to endow the market with social regulation functions as if, according to the theory of comparative advantages, the progression of the goods and services trade was eventually going to reduce areas of poverty and thus ease peripheral political and social conflicts. In the long run, the free functioning of the market is supposed to produce wealth and well-being.

Some of the poor countries are torn apart by conflictual violence and civil wars with an increasingly strong ethnic dimension. By definition civil war entails the destruction of the most basic institutional conditions necessary to the protection of human rights. We usually associate civil wars and repressive regimes with internal phenomena but as a matter of fact they are generally influenced by international politics, even when they appear to have a strong endogenous origin. Indeed, these wars reveal not only the collapse of state integration structures, but also the failure of international cooperation mechanisms. In the 1990s civil wars broke out in countries going through severe social crises, heavily indebted with international financial institutions, private banks, and Western governments. Events in Yugoslavia are proof of this. In the months preceding the crisis and outbreak of war, the IMF demanded that, in return for new loans, the Yugoslav authorities set up a programme of budgetary austerity measures and economic liberalization, which led to recession and an increase in unemployment, while demanding that the different member states of the Federation carry out economic and political reforms that they could not accept. Civil wars and genocides in Africa have stricken countries undergoing profound socio-economic crises, partly determined by international constraints such as the degradation of their terms of trade and the diminution of economic assistance. At the same time, in the 1990s, OECD countries noticeably reduced the size of their development assistance of which a significant steadily increasing chunk is concentrated on humanitarian operations.

Failures of International Institutions

International organizations are mandated to support cooperation regimes in the socio-economic or political domains that states cannot manage independently. Their expansion is wrongly associated with the erosion of national sovereignty, whereas their mission should be to support a state's capacity to fulfil its main functions in terms of security and welfare. As a matter of fact, the divide between the states' level of development also reflects a difference in the nature and solidity of their regional or international cooperation mechanisms whose intergovernmental institutions are an important instrument. OECD countries have reached a high degree of socio-economic and political integration among themselves. This is even more so within the European Union. However, international society as a whole is characterized by the weakness and heterogeneity of its cooperation regimes.

The UN system, which has played an important role in the definition of the norms and strategies related to human rights and development, has lacked the political support from its member states the major powers in particular and consequently the financial resources necessary to contribute significantly to the socio-economic progress of poor countries. The atmosphere at these conferences was more serene than in the past thanks to the absence of the major ideological rifts of the Cold War era. Nonetheless, their final recommendations formed a long list of proposals that governments could not or did not intend to respect. Moreover, the financial resources committed by states to achieve the objectives set up within these conferences have remained very limited.

The United States have constantly sidelined the United Nations from vital development matters: the price of raw materials, debt, trade, financial and monetary matters. They consider the United Nations should play a marginal role in economic and social areas even if they do attach some importance to humanitarian affairs, particularly regarding the flow of refugees, which comes under the UNHCR mandate. European Union countries' governments and public opinion have not really resisted this policy. The heterogeneity of UN membership, the complexity of its structure and its cumbersome decision-making process can explain the rich countries' indifference to this system. Furthermore, conference diplomacy where representatives of each government expose their points of view and painstakingly produce the long list of often unrealistic and contradictory recommendations is a strikingly unsuitable negotiation procedure for defining consistent development strategies. The practice of consensus for adopting a set of recommendations has resulted in further weakening the significance and weight of UN decisions. For these reasons, UN organizations contribute little to international social regulation.

They are certainly not in a position to carry out effectively their mandate to defend the social and economic rights of poor peoples. Since the collapse of the Bretton Woods monetary system at the beginning of the seventies up until fairly recently, the IMF and the World Bank have been of little help in facilitating coordination of rich countries' macro-economic policies to guarantee stability in exchange rates, avoid financial crises and encourage the development of poor countries as well as resolve the haunting problem of their debt. Instead of improving the situation, these institutions often contributed in the past to the social crisis of developing countries by supporting policies that condemned millions of human beings to a life of misery and grave violations of human rights. At the same time the development strategies recommended by these institutions were not being successful either. As a rule their policy triggered a high level of unemployment and increased inequality. A recent study on Latin America by the World Bank highlights this paradox: over the past years countries in the region have gone to great lengths to comply with IMF and World Bank directions, carrying out macro-economic reforms and major structural changes. They have taken steps to liberalize their economy, to open their markets to international competition, reducing their customs tariffs on average from 50 per cent in 1985 to 10 per cent in 1996, to reduce or eliminate their budgetary deficit, to modify their monetary policy, to liberalize their financial market and reform their banking system, to limit considerably their inflation rate and reform their social security system. Inflation is practically non-existent now and yet all this progress and resulting growth has done nothing to alleviate the glaring social injustices or reduce the number of poor. By the early 1990s the number of poor people had soared to 150 million. Yet according to the Bank another effort had to be made, particularly by reducing workers' social protection to facilitate lay-offs and by reducing employers' social security contributions.

As a matter of fact the IMF and the World Bank continue to propose development strategies which take no account of human rights as proclaimed by the United Nations and the treaties ratified by states on the subject. The incoherence of World Bank projects in this respect has become unquestionable. In fact, its proclaimed principles and ideals in favour of social progress particularly for family planning, basic health care, education, housing and employment or environment are often undermined by the nature of the structural adjustment policy it recommends or imposes. Inspired by neo-classic conceptions, these measures are implemented regardless of the economic specificities of the different indebted countries, or even of the social conditions in the countries concerned. The debt burden of many poor countries is still exorbitant, whereas the liberalization of African economies has in no way slackened the region's drift away from the main poles of production and trade.

Moreover the IMF, under the aegis of the American Treasury Department, urged developing countries to liberalize movements of capital when they did not have the institutional means to assume this deregulation. During the autumn of 1997, the IMF was unable to do anything to prevent a series of competitive devaluations between the newly industrialized Asian countries. It nonetheless granted important loans to the governments of Thailand, Indonesia, and South Korea, while imposing austerity measures on the same governments. These measures were strongly criticized, even by the most ardent supporters of the free-market economy. In exchange for loans, the IMF imposed measures on these countries' governments similar to those which had been applied in indebted countries during the eighties, whereas such measures were unnecessary in this context and contributed to aggravating the monetary crisis. The IMF also demanded that these governments lift or reduce their restrictions on foreign investors' rights regarding national companies; this deregulation was bound to favour foreign banks and corporations. The structural adjustment measures recommended by Bretton Woods organizations have always been selective: they never aimed measures at rich countries' trade and monetary policies. These shortcomings reflect both their dependence on great economic powers and their technocratic working methods.

As we have seen, the World Bank appears today very interested in "good governance" involving respect for law, justice, and constitutional norms and procedures which render governments accountable for their actions. In 1993 the Bank established an Inspection Panel to provide an independent forum for private citizens who believe that they or their interests have been or could be directly harmed by a project that it finances. Moreover it recently suspended granting a loan to Indonesia by way of a sanction for a corruption affair involving a bank in Bali, but also for the central government's refusal to respect referendum results in East Timor. Yet this interest has not prevented James Wolfensohn from paying tribute to President Putin at the time of the war in Chechnya.

It should be added that all too often international institutions escape some of the basic principles of "good governance," in particular the check-and-balance mechanisms necessary for the functioning of democratic institutions. They are the seats for negotiations that often take place in the greatest secrecy under the aegis of the major economic powers supported by business circles. They avoid control by national parliaments because of their technical nature and sometimes their decisions affect the fate of millions of individuals with large-scale social and ecological consequences. They have expanded their programmes and policies in the last decades without becoming accountable to those whom they directly concern. As Philip Alston, Chairman of the Committee for Economic, Social and Cultural Rights, stated in 1998: "The IMF decides on the economic future of entire populations without being accountable to them in any way." Besides this it demands "complete transparency on the monetary policy that states intend to elaborate while the Fund itself continues to prepare its structural adjustment measures in the utmost secrecy." Globalization has resulted in increased segmentation of the roles played by international institutions. Thus the WTO has been given a far-reaching mandate regarding the liberalization of goods and services. It has received wide-ranging competence for developing this regime of liberalization. It has a dispute settlement body, which appears to be functioning efficiently for the time being. Protection of the environment, respect for human rights and social rights, and the objectives of sustainable development are all subject to respect of the WTO obligations. In fact, no international institution exists with such extensive legal and judicial means necessary to impose enforcement of its sector-based aims.

The acceleration of liberalization generated by the implementation of WTO objectives might well result in a widening of the social rift unless states and international institutions take measures to correct markets' adverse effects. The constitution of the WTO contains no clause on social protection apart from a vague reference in the preamble to the relations between the easing of restrictions on trade and full employment. States cannot ban importation of products manufactured by children because the WTO condemns discriminatory treatment on the basis of national production methods, with the exception of work done by prisoners.

The WTO Ministerial Conference, held in Singapore from 9–13 December 1996, released the Organization from all competence in social matters, proposing that ILO assume its mandate in this respect an elegant way of giving in to pressure from developing countries and transnational corporations who refuse to address this matter. Not without reason, governments of Southern countries consider that the increased interest on the part of OECD countries for the social dimensions of development or the environment is a protectionist strategy. They particularly believe that the low level of their social protection mechanism is one of their comparative advantages. In the North and South alike, supporters of the neo-liberal-inspired economic model are hostile to the idea of establishing social protection norms at the international level. They fear that the setting up of some sort of an international social regulation system would raise labour costs, favour public debt and lead to an increase in interest rates. Increased trade will encourage economic growth in developing countries and this growth will lead to a rise in their imports from OECD countries and improved working conditions. The ILO secretariat defends the idea of a mechanism sanctioning violations of certain of the Organization's fundamental clauses such as the banning of forced labour, child labour, freedom of trade unions and discrimination in the workplace. Some member states, however, including the United States, have not signed the Organization's conventions in these areas. This is why, in November 1997, the ILO's Governing Body proposed obtaining a consensus on a Declaration by the International Labour Conference reaffirming the essential principles of these conventions. This only goes to show how difficult it is now to implement vital norms on the international protection of workers.

The Role of Non-state Actors

It is widely accepted nowadays that non-state actors contribute to economic and social regulation. Private corporations contribute to rule making or to the setting of all kind of standards, for example in telecommunications, food, medicine, finance, insurance, labour, or environment. Private enterprises are often considered to be more efficient, less bureaucratic and more sensitive to the requirements of change. The irruption of private actors in the public sphere could also account for governmental shortcomings. Yet integrating transnational corporations into governance structures implies enhancing the status of their contribution to political order or at least their economic and social role. They also contribute to deregulation in the economic and social sphere. Some transnational corporations, especially multinational oil companies, have also recently been accomplices to human rights violations. The civil wars or repression in several African or Asian countries would not have lasted so long nor been so far-reaching without the collusion of the transnational corporations which exploit these bankrupt states' petroleum resources. In any case, the delegitimization of nation states through the action of transnational corporations and capital flow is not necessarily an expression of good governance. It is not always conducive to a better protection of human rights.

The irruption on the political scene of NGOs and all sorts of local and regional networks of associations is also a long way from resolving the question of procedure for democratic political participation. Human rights organizations and even development NGOs have little direct access to the WTO and the IMF whereas they have more and more representatives within international fora whose political influence is limited. They form nevertheless heterogeneous coalitions to protest against the policies pursued by OECD countries under the aegis of the organizations, expressing in this way the emergence of a new transnational public space.

Consumer movements can also contribute to demanding new codes of conduct by transnational corporations for the protection of the environment, or even for the protection of specific social rights.

In human rights matters NGOs are most of the time used to protesting against violations of individual liberties and serious breaches of human dignity perpetrated by governments, but they have not yet developed a concerted strategy to challenge private corporations which turn out to be accomplices to these violations. Moreover NGOs would be wise to devote more energy to pushing through reform of international institutions by again raising the issues of sovereignty and legitimacy, namely who is entitled to give the orders, according to which mode, submitting to which control body and within the framework of which political participation structure.

A Programme for Change

Progress in the implementation of human rights will not ensue from new legal international instruments, or from lofty rhetoric about individual liberty and democracy, but from the mobilization of political forces willing to fight mass poverty and to improve governance at the national and international level. Misery and social polarizations all over the world are today a major obstacle to the realization of human rights. They contribute to insecurity and violence, sometimes to civil war, which are an absolute hindrance to the rule of law. There can be no stable political order either where there is no respect for the most elementary conditions of equity, justice, and social integration.

The scope and gravity of worldwide social problems necessitates in particular the development of new systems of regulation and a better control of present institutions. It is obvious that the state is no longer the sole authority which should be held accountable for violations of human rights, especially of economic and social rights. By strengthening their cooperation systems and sharing their sovereignty within the framework of regional integration structures, states should be in a better position to bear their responsibilities in fighting unemployment and developing new social protection systems. In any case, states will have to take measures to curb the concentration of economic power that can be seen in the spheres of banking and transnational corporations. They will have to harmonize their monetary policies and their social demands regarding these corporations and to restrain short-term movements of capital.

It seems particularly necessary to set up a new financial architecture. Solutions will have to be found quickly to the phenomenon of the poorest countries' massive debt. The IMF's mandate should be enlarged, so that, as John Maynard Keynes proposed at Bretton Woods, its stabilization and adjustment programmes are not directed exclusively against indebted countries. In any case, the IMF should be more sensitive to people's standard of living and abandon its obsession with the stabilization of the financial market and the fight against inflation in order to enhance responsibility for employment and sustainable development. It is becoming urgent to integrate social policy into development strategies. The progress of poor countries cannot be measured with the yardstick of criteria such as capital flow and easing of trade restrictions or the competitively of their economies in the world market.

The beneficial objective of easing restrictions on the goods and services trade will have to be subject to the requirements of political order and the common good. Developing countries will have to take measures in order to regulate short-term capital movements that can trigger major socio-economic crises. They should resume policies aiming at the protection of their infant industries. They should promote the establishment of a world investment fund whose main function would be to assist the development of poor countries and which would be financed through a new international fiscal system such as the Tobin tax. The

WTO, or any other organization, should be mandated to supervise transnational corporations whose oligopolistic structure is a threat to competition. Human rights have little chance of progressing on a universal basis in a world where governments have to give into the interests of transnational corporations and private financial institutions or to the erratic constraints of speculative movements of capital. When capitalism is not regulated it finally destroys all principles of political and social organization. This is why the promotion of human rights is a political struggle which should be pursued not only at the national level, but also within the public space of international society.

3

Universal Human Rights

Introduction

The violence of the French Revolution, and various social, economic and intellectual developments of the late eighteenth and early nineteenth centuries led to the discrediting of the concept of natural rights. Science-based philosophies, knowledge of diverse cultures, a new emphasis on historical evolution and the rise of nationalism were among the cultural forces that called the very idea of a universal morality into question. The doctrines of natural law and natural rights were, nevertheless, maintained throughout the nineteenth and early twentieth centuries by international lawyers and some liberal philosophers. After the Second World War, when the victorious powers sought to establish a new world order on the moral basis of the condemnation of Nazism and Fascism, the fashionable philosophies of the time positivism, utilitarianism and existentialism were ill-suited to the task. The principles of universal human rights loosely derived from the moral and political philosophies of Locke and Kant were the best available ethical resources to express the values that Nazism and Fascism had violated. The victors of the war perceived themselves to have been engaged in a global struggle, and it seemed natural, therefore, that their post-war declarations of principles in particular, the United Nations Charter and the Universal Declaration of Human Rights should claim to have universal validity. Thus, the global character of the United Nations as a political organization was underpinned by a universalist ethic that derived from the French Revolution, Christian universalism and natural-law philosophy. The idea of universal human rights, therefore, had a definite, particular and historically contingent political and philosophical basis.

More or less contemporaneous with these globalizing and universalist developments were certain tendencies in world politics that would turn out to call the idea of universal human rights into question. The anti-colonial revolution struck out against the weakened European imperial powers, and was successful almost everywhere in the three decades after the war. At first, this revolution seemed consistent with UN universalism, for the anti-colonial movement was based on the principle of national self-determination, which had been enshrined in the UN Charter; the new, post-colonial states wished to join the UN club; and they appeared to accept its principles, including those of universal human rights. Tensions then began to develop between the post-colonial states, which were generally poor, and the major Western powers, which were relatively rich. This North-South divide was, however, dominated by the East-West divide of the Cold War. When Eastern-European Communism collapsed in the period 1989-91, it was widely expected that the North-South divide would become more salient in world politics, and pervade debates about human rights. Unexpectedly, certain leaders of the economically successful societies of South-East Asia seized the initiative, and took the opportunity presented by the UN World Conference on Human Rights that was held in Vienna in June 1993 to assert the propriety of culturally diverse interpretations of human rights principles. Western liberals, having won their ideological struggle with Marxism, were faced with a new challenge to the idea of universal human rights. At the end of 1997 the 'Asian tigers' experienced an economic crisis. It is not possible to foresee the long-term economic or political consequences of this crisis. Whatever these may be, the Asian challenge to the idea of universal human rights merits careful reflection on the relation between universal ethical claims and the requirements of particular cultures.

The Stoic conception of the two cities the local and the universal - has to be reconsidered in late twentieth-century circumstances. Is the idea of 'universal human rights' a manifestation of Western hegemony and/or of cultural imperialism? Is the idea of culturally particular interpretations of human rights a thin veil, behind which gross abuses of state power will take place? The problem is both political and philosophical. Human rights constitutes a terrain both of struggles between states, and of struggles within states between governments and oppositions. Philosophically, the ethical claims of local and national communities, on the one hand, and of humanity as such, on the other hand, have been the subject of intense debate. As Humanity has disputed with Culture, the question has arisen as to who are the legitimate representatives of these parties. Is the UN the authoritative representative of humanity? Are governments the authoritative representatives of their peoples? Has the debate about human rights been a dispute between ' Asia' and 'the West', or has the assertion of 'Asian values' against the claims of human rights universalism been a new affirmation of *conservative* objections to 'rights-talk' that could be found in both Asia and the West?

The concepts of 'Asian values' and 'human rights' are culturally embedded, but this proposition begs important questions about the internal structure and dynamics of cultures. 'Cultures' are not 'things' to pick up and inspect. They are complex, contested and mutable. The boundaries of cultures are neither fixed nor clear, and do not necessarily coincide with those of states. Cultures interpret human experience, and experiences can be shared by peoples in different societies and different cultures. Cultural systems, such as that of the human rights doctrine, can, therefore, make sense and have ethical force across state borders and traditional cultural boundaries. The adoption of such cosmopolitan cultural elements into local situations is itself always likely to be contested. These contests will not only be between those 'inside' the culture and those 'outside'. They will also be among those who are 'inside'. The modern institution of the nation-state and the processes of global capitalism have set similar problems to peoples in different societies with different cultural traditions. The claim that the human rights concept has universal validity proposes a common set of minimum conditions, not for a world of cultural uniformity, as is often charged and feared, but for the world's peoples to meet these challenges and achieve a life of dignity. The aim of this chapter is to assess the ethical force of this claim.

Culture and Interpretation

The Vienna Declaration re-affirmed the principle that all human rights are universal, but qualified this by stating that 'the significance of national and regional particularities and various historical, cultural and religious backgrounds must be borne in mind'. Thus, this authoritative UN text left unresolved the relation between the universality of human rights and the legitimacy of culturally particular conceptions of human rights. The debate about human rights and Asian values is only one manifestation of this more general problem. The vigorous defence of Asian values by certain Asian elites in contemporary international affairs is an example of what has been called 'the revolt against the West', a term that expresses not only the resistance of colonial and post-colonial societies to colonial and 'neo-colonial' domination, but also the political re-assertion of the value of non-Western cultures that have been subjected to centuries of Western economic, political and cultural hegemony.

The principle of the universality of human rights and the affirmation of the value of Asian cultural difference might be reconciled, and a distinctively Asian conception of human rights might also be defended, by pointing out that the principles of human rights are quite general, and must be both *interpreted* and *applied* in particular situations. The principles of human rights, so this argument goes, are 'thin', highly indeterminate and unclear, unless and until they are interpreted in terms of the different cultures that are the sources of 'thick' social meaning for the diverse peoples of the world. There is, therefore, necessarily a diversity of interpretations of human rights. The principles of human rights will seem plausible, also, only if their interpretation takes into account the diverse *circumstances,* such as the level of economic development, in which the peoples of the world struggle for survival and a life of dignity. To apply abstract, putatively universal principles to particular situations, it may plausibly be argued, without taking into account the specificities cultural, economic, political and military of those situations is morally and politically irresponsible.

However, to affirm that the interpretation and application of human rights principles require us to take account of different cultures and circumstances begs the question of *how* these cultures and circumstances are themselves to be interpreted, and *by whom.* Cultural values are logically similar to human rights standards in that they are often formulated as general principles. Michael Carrithers has argued that popular cultures are often 'narrative' rather than 'paradigmatic' (systems of general principles). This is an important consideration, especially since the pervasive Western predilection for expressing the principles of human rights in a juridical discourse leads to strongly paradigmatic forms of representation. Both Yash Ghai and Joseph Chan have suggested that this form of representation can produce resistance in Asian cultural settings. However, it should be pointed out that Asian values are often represented paradigmatically and, as Amnesty International has discovered, the narrative representation of human rights violations can be effective transculturally. The problem of how general principles should be interpreted and applied in particular situations, therefore, is raised by appeals to cultural values as it is by appeals to human rights. We should, therefore, ask who is morally and epistemologically competent to interpret the diverse cultures of the world.

A common answer that is given to this question in international politics is that *governments* represent their *peoples,* or, put differently, *states* represent *nations* (the concept of the 'nation-state' and the United Nations Charter both make this assumption) and that 'outsiders', i.e. those not citizens of the nation-state in question, should presume that governments speak for their peoples, unless this is obviously not the case, for example, in situations of persistent civil war or massive human rights violations, such as genocide. One of the most frequent defences against charges of human rights violations in international politics is not to deny the universality of human rights in principle, but to affirm that the interpretation and application of universal human rights principles are exclusively internal concerns of nation-states and that governments are protected from interference from outsiders concerned about alleged human-rights violations by the doctrine of state sovereignty. The principle of state sovereignty is, of course, a key element of the conception of the international order that is enshrined in the United Nations Charter. This conception is derived from the 'Westphalian' system (named after the Peace of Westphalia, 1648), according to which states recognize each other's sovereign authority over their own territories and their populations, and the equal legal status of each vis-a-vis each other internationally. The principle of state sovereignty is important because its primary *raison d'être* is to maintain peace and co operative relations among states, and, insofar as it contributes to those ends, it has considerable moral and political weight. However, it is not appropriately applied to the interpretation of cultures. It is true that, according to Thomas Hobbes' classic theory of sovereignty, the state, which has the overriding obligation to maintain social peace, may determine the interpretation of culture where this is necessary to avoid social conflict. However, Hobbes' theory was a *universalist* proposal for the establishment of social peace, and was not motivated by a concern to respect cultural diversity. Whatever the merits of this theory may be, it cannot be used to support the idea of a distinctively Asian conception of human rights.

Culture, Democracy and Human Rights

Some governments may claim that the cultural traditions of their societies legitimate the role of governments as interpreters of culture, but acceptance of such claims without further investigation begs the question at issue: who is competent to interpret the tradition? The requirement that we respect cultural differences, therefore, obliges us to reject the claim that governments are necessarily the most reliable interpreters of the cultural values of the people whom they govern. Traditionally, the primary functions of government have been the maintenance of internal order and external defence. In some cases, and in some political theories, the government has a role in promoting the 'virtue' of the people. In modern times, states have taken on the functions of economic management and social welfare. The interpretation of cultures, however, has not commonly been thought to be the business of government. Even in authoritarian, conservative societies, this task has been allocated to specialized elites, such as priests, officials and intellectuals. Governmental elites in modern, socially differentiated nation-states are not only often culturally distinct from many of the people whom they govern (for example, Chinese Communists and Tibetans; anglophone and francophone elites in Canada and 'first nations'), but they also commonly adopt policies (for example, of rapid economic development) that undermine in various ways the cultural values of their peoples (for example, by putting economic pressure on family bonds and/or opening the society to outside cultural influences). Therefore, although cultural outsiders should be cautious in attempting to 'second-guess' governments in their interpretations of the cultures of their peoples, they are obliged to attend to the voice of the people as it expresses its real culture.

No account of the relation between the universality of human rights and the particularity of cultures can be plausible without an analysis of precisely what 'cultures' are and why they have value. For this purpose, I shall take the term 'culture' to refer to the beliefs, values, norms, sentiments and practices that support, give meaning and (at least in favourable cases) value to human lives. This definition is wholly neutral between Asian and Western cultures. It is also neutral between 'individualist' and 'collectivist' cultures. The *content* of beliefs, values, norms, sentiments and practices varies from one culture to another. But beliefs, values, norms, sentiments and practices are universal features of culture. Let us now ask who is most competent, morally and epistemologically, to *interpret* the beliefs, values, norms, sentiments and practices of a particular culture. The question nearly answers itself. Those are most competent to interpret a culture who believe the beliefs, value the values, endorse the norms, feel the sentiments, and engage in the practices, and who must live the consequences of their interpretations. In other words, the most competent interpreters of a culture are those whose culture it actually is.

It follows from this that respect for cultural diversity, which is often represented as a problem for the principle of the universality of human rights, may, quite to the contrary, require the robust implementation of that principle. For, if we should respect the diversity of cultures, and if the most reliable interpreters of the diverse cultures of the world are those whose cultures they really are, we are obliged to adopt a *democratic* conception of cultural interpretation. We cannot respect cultures unless we have reliable knowledge of what those cultures are, and we cannot have reliable knowledge of cultures unless the voice of the people is clearly heard. Many individuals and groups throughout history have claimed to speak for 'the people', but we have theoretical and empirical grounds for being quite sceptical of such claims. Theoretically, elites may well lack the capacity to understand the culture of the people and may also lack the incentive to understand it. Empirically, we know that elites have commonly been unconcerned with, or hostile to the culture of the people. The voice of the people is the expression of culture, and the voice of the people cannot be heard unless all the people have a secure set of rights. If some of the people, for example, are not free from the fear of arbitrary arrest, or if women are excluded from public life, then it is not the voice of the people that will be heard, and we cannot reliably know whether the culture of the people is being truly represented.

Just as discussion of the relation between universal human rights and cultural diversity is distorted by the assumption that governments necessarily speak for the cultures of their peoples, so it is also confused by an oversimplified conception of the relations between 'peoples' and 'cultures'. For, if 'cultures' consist of general beliefs and rules that have to be interpreted and applied in particular circumstances, it is clear that actual cultures must be complex, contested and constantly changing. Even if an individual holds an apparently fixed belief (for example, in the duty of the individual to promote the good of the community) the precise meaning of this belief necessarily varies for that individual from one situation to another. Individuals can also experience doubts about even their most cherished beliefs. If this is true for *individuals*, it is true *a fortiori* for groups. A group may appear to hold a fixed belief for example, in the value of 'economic development' but different individuals within that group may interpret that belief differently. Under contemporary conditions, in which most human individuals and groups are subject to dynamic forces that are, to a considerable extent, beyond their control (for example, market prices for the goods that they produce, or the dissemination of alien cultures), the instability of beliefs held by individuals and by groups is likely to be great. As a consequence, even groups that appear to outsiders to be culturally homogeneous, and that may be presented to outsiders by their own leaders as culturally homogeneous, are likely to contain *internal* diversity. In other words, the concept of 'cultural diversity' does not refer us to a definite number of externally diverse, but internally homogeneous cultural groups. Still less does it refer us to the *nation-states* or *regions* of the world, but it leads us to a complex web of relatively unstable beliefs, values, norms, sentiments and practices. This is not to deny that some human groups may have *relatively* well-defined and distinctive cultures that sustain the lives of their members. It may well be, for example, that there are certain socially and ethically important, distinctively Chinese cultural characteristics that are shared by ethnic Chinese living in different nation-states. But we should guard against the assumption that what are commonly called 'cultures', as if they were a well-defined and distinctive kind of 'thing', are homogeneous and uncontentious to those people whose cultures they undoubtedly are.

All cultural groups face the problem of how to adapt to the rapid technological, cultural, economic and political changes that pervade the contemporary world. Most of them experience tensions between those who favour relatively 'traditionalist' and those who favour relatively 'modernizing' solutions. The distinction between 'traditionalists' and 'modernizers' cuts right across the categories of 'Asian' and 'Western' cultures, and those who seek some optimal combination of the traditional and the modern are to be found in both Asia and the West. All governments are committed to economic modernization, and this has, historically, been associated with increasingly strong and active states and/ or dynamic markets. The idea of human rights was developed to protect certain putatively universal human interests against the most threatening features of modernization. Yet, although modernization commonly (though not necessarily) entails the emergence of the human-rights idea, that idea can protect many (though not all) traditional practices where such protection is necessary for human well-being.

Exchange and Domination

The problem of Asian values and human rights may be further clarified by use of the concepts of 'exchange' and 'domination'. Let us begin with two simple examples. If I give you a gift, and you give me a gift, and we are both pleased with our gifts, we are both winners, and a satisfying exchange has taken place. If, however, you *impose* something on me against my will, the relation between us will be oppressive to me, *however well-intentioned your action was.* If, for example, you force me to participate in a cultural practice which is extremely valuable to you, but meaningless and even perhaps unpleasant to me, this is *unjust domination* not *free exchange.*

These examples employ abstract agents and assume that exchange takes place between equal parties to their mutual advantage. Empirically, anthropologists have shown that exchanges are governed by cultural norms. These norms may make exchanges into forms of domination: superior parties may manipulate the norms to their advantage. This raises persistent philosophical questions about whether altruism is reducible to self-interest. These are important empirical and conceptual issues. They do not, however, undermine the value of distinguishing between equal and mutual advantageous exchange, on the one hand, and domination, on the other hand, *as ideal typical relations* in order to analyse the xenophobic claim that cultural imports are *necessarily* harmful to the importing society.

Throughout history peoples have engaged in cultural exchanges. They have traded useful and beautiful goods and learned useful and inspiring ideas from each other. Such exchanges enrich both sides. Throughout history also, however, some peoples have *dominated* others through imperialistic expansion, for example often from self-interested and therefore exploitative motives, but sometimes from benevolent intentions. Benevolent domination may be quite as oppressive as self-interested exploitation. If one people dominates another in order to 'civilize' them, they do not necessarily treat them with more justice than if they dominate the other in order to make money out of them.

In modern history Western peoples have dominated others, often for the purpose of self-interested exploitation, and, even when from benevolent motives, often unjustly and oppressively. Asian peoples have often been the victims of this oppressive and unjust Western domination. It is understandable that Asian people should resent this domination, and right that they should seek to liberate themselves from its harmful consequences. The resistance of some Asians to the concept of human rights, or the desire of some Asians to have *their own conception* of human rights, appears to be part of this process of self-emancipation from Western domination. Asian-state elites and peoples have generally, and in various ways, adopted strategies of selective imitation of the West. Western technology is generally adopted enthusiastically, but attitudes to Western culture are commonly ambivalent. The concept of human rights is caught to some extent in this ambivalence. The humanity of human rights is consonant to a considerable extent with widely held Asian religious, moral and political values, but, nevertheless, the concept of 'human rights' itself appears to 'come out of the West', as the 'black ships' of imperialism once did, bringing alien and overbearing demands to Asian lands yet again. In this perspective, the concept of 'universality' appears to be a thin disguise for Western cultural (and perhaps political and economic) domination. This perception of the concept of human rights is not without irony, because the political role of the concept in Western history has been precisely to articulate *opposition to unjust domination.* Although Western imperialism has been justified historically in the name of certain supposed rights (the right to civilize, the rights of free trade, for example) the struggle against imperialism has also appealed to human rights, especially the right to self-determination.

A Global Community

However, in order to defend themselves against Western domination, the non-Western peoples have adopted certain Western institutions and projects. They have, for example, constituted themselves politically in neo-Westphalian nation-states, since this form of political community is a necessary condition of effective membership of the global political and economic systems. They have also committed themselves to the project of national economic development, which is universally seen as the precondition both of general well-being and of external influence. The specific forms of the nation-state and the specific strategies of economic development are, of course, highly varied, shaped by historical experiences, especially those of colonialism, and by the dynamics of global socio-economic forces. However, notwithstanding the great political and economic, structural and strategic diversity that characterizes social relations in the contemporary global arena, the institution of the nation-state and the project of economic development have become universalized. But, as weapons of defence against unjust domination, nation-states and economic development are double edged swords. They were achieved in the West by the oppression (and sometimes the extermination) of some cultural groups by aggressive modernizers. Similarly, in the non-Western world, they can be at the same time means to construct defences against Western hegemony and instruments for the oppression or destruction of cultures.

All human beings now live in a world that consists of many different kinds of cultural group: small, relatively isolated tribes; modern or modernizing nations; religious communities that transcend the borders of nation-states; professional, political or humanitarian networks in which individuals communicate with each other in cyberspace. The diverse individuals, cultural groups and states that interact in complex ways on this technologically shrunken planet have an unprecedented capacity to affect each other's well-being, for good or ill. The people of the globe constitute a moral community, *not* in the sense that they share a common moral culture, for they clearly do not, but in the sense that they *need* a *minimal* (though rather robust) common code, *so that all can flourish in their own, diverse ways.* The concept of the universality of human rights recognizes the vulnerability of *every human being* to disabling and degrading suffering and the capacity of each to contribute to the continuing maintenance, negotiation and reconstruction of local and national cultures, and thereby to the common global good.

Such rights as those to freedom from arbitrary arrest and freedom from torture, and those to freedom of religion, speech, association and participation in the culture of one's community are designed to empower persons and collectivities to engage in social relations locally, nationally, globally so that the cultural interactions of individuals, groups and nations should have, as far as possible, the character of mutually enriching, free exchange, and, as little as possible, that of unjust domination. Individual human rights (such as freedom of association and freedom of religion, for example) can, therefore, *protect* cultural communities, and vibrant cultural communities can *enrich* our conceptions of human rights. The principle of universal human rights can, of course, conflict with the requirements of local cultures, but conflicts of principles are commonly found *within* cultural, moral and political systems, whether they aspire to be universal or are narrowly particularistic.

Dialogue and Beyond

Those who argue for a distinctively 'Asian' conception of human rights sometimes, to show the reasonableness of their position, call for a 'dialogue' on human rights. The call for dialogue appears unobjectionable. It is important to inquire, however, who is to participate in this dialogue. If the issue is posed as one between 'Asian values' and 'Western values', the dialogue proposed is likely to be one among *governments* that supposedly represent those values. Governments may, of course, properly conduct dialogues about human rights. But a dialogue of governments about Asian and Western values assumes both the validity of these categories and the competence of governments to represent those values. I have argued that both assumptions are dangerously misleading. The democratic and complex conception of culture that I have defended requires a continuing dialogue on human rights that is not monopolized by governments. There is a paradox that, unless certain human rights are secure, *no effective dialogue about human rights can take place.* People who are starving, illiterate, persecuted or excluded from public life cannot take part effectively in dialogues about their rights. There are, of course, difficult questions about how everyone can achieve the material and psychological level necessary for effective participation in dialogue, including questions of economic development strategies and of international justice. But, if it is common ground that everyone is entitled, so far as possible, to a life of at least minimal material and spiritual well-being, it would be more fruitful to tackle the obstacles to this goal than to continue distracting debates about regional interpretations of human rights. Advocates of universal human rights can contribute to eliminating such distractions by developing a sensitivity to the particular cultural style in which they speak to representatives of other cultures about human rights, and to the difficult histories that all societies have passed through in their search for greater justice. They should also be careful not to present the doctrine of human rights as a sort of fundamentalist religion. The idea of human rights is more accurately and plausibly presented as a set of necessary, minimum standards for everyone to lead a life of dignity.

Joseph Chan has suggested that the human rights which are preconditions for dialogue might be few, such as freedom of speech and association. I would counter that more human rights may be necessary for genuine dialogue, including, for example, freedom from arbitrary arrest and from significant forms of social discrimination. It is important, however, to distinguish *the grounds of human rights from the preconditions of dialogue.* The ethical force of human rights depends on a plausible conception of human dignity or human flourishing. Consequently, human rights are designed to protect a wide range of human interests. All human beings have an interest in participating in dialogues about their rights, and therefore have an interest in securing recognition of those rights that are preconditions to such participation, but this particular interest, important though it is, is far from being the only interest to be protected by human rights. The need to interpret human rights principles requires dialogue. Genuine dialogue requires the protection of certain human rights. Thus, paradoxically, rights and dialogue seem to be preconditions for each other. There is no simple way to resolve this paradox. It is plausible to suggest, however, that the stronger the rights of the participants, the more genuine is the dialogue, but recognition of the controversial character of some rights interpretations is also a necessary condition of genuine dialogue.

Summary

Western human rights liberals can both understand and support these general goals, while pressing the case for seeking to reconcile 'development' (in the sense of improving the quality of life on the basis of a reasonable conception of social justice) with democracy and human rights. The idea of universal human rights is a modern, conceptual invention, the purpose of which is to create global solidarity in the struggle against injustice. It was inspired to a large extent by revulsion against the evils of Nazism. It produced an extensive consensus in the campaign against apartheid. Its future is uncertain, but it will certainly be controversial. Chan has stated one of the central problems of claims to the universality of human rights with admirable succinctness. 'The formulas contained in the human rights charters are merely short hands for arguments; it is not the formulas that make sense of human rights, but the arguments behind them'. This is a cogent point from a philosophical point of view. It ignores, however, the *legal* status of human rights principles, and the *ethical* status of international law. There is a clear and urgent need for further philosophical reflection on the relations among the international law of human rights, the human rights policies of governments and the 'real' cultures of peoples.

Controversies about human rights will, therefore, almost certainly persist, but they will persist *within* all societies, and differences *within* societies about the interpretation and application of human rights may remain quite as important as differences *among* societies. In the continuing debate about the interpretation and application of human rights it is not likely that such sweeping, general concepts as 'Asian values' or 'Western values' will give us much help. They are more likely to be smokescreens behind which those with power indulge their traditional appetite for exploitation and oppression.

Because the doctrine of human rights sets only minimum standards, it should not be used to solve all the complex moral, political and economic problems of contemporary societies. To overstretch the concept of human rights is to weaken it. Because the concept seeks to empower human individuals in complex and highly diverse situations, it is not helpful to retain in our dialogue on human rights what have aptly been called the 'tired dichotomies' of East and West, community and individual, rights and duties. *All* societies have to balance the interests of individuals and of communities, and rights with duties. *All* societies are likely to find complex solutions to these problems, and, in *all* societies, these balances will shift over time in the face of changing circumstances. The rigid dichotomization of 'Asian' and 'Western' approaches to these problems is not likely to clarify what is actually going on in these societies nor which solutions will best serve the needs of their peoples.

Confucius said: 'If you do not know a person's speech, you cannot understand him'. We cannot afford to ignore this piece of universal wisdom. And, if you do not understand a person, you cannot treat that person justly. The conversation of mankind must continue, and no-one should be excluded from it. If we formulate our problems in terms of a 'clash of civilizations', as Samuel Huntington has notoriously suggested, we shall find ourselves, in the vivid phrase of Claus Offe, in the tunnel at the end of the light.

4

Universal Human Rights and Asian Values

Introduction

Vietnam first entered the 'Asian values' debate at the Bangkok Regional Preparatory Meeting to the Vienna World Conference on Human Rights in 1993. Although Vietnam had formally accepted the principles of universality by acceding to UN human rights instruments such as the International Covenants on Civil and Political Rights and Economic, Social and Cultural Rights in 1982, its delegation nevertheless stated at Bangkok that 'there exists no ready-to-serve formula for human rights that can be imported or, worse still, imposed successfully from outside'. Along with 49 Asian countries, Vietnam signed the 1993 Bangkok Declaration which emphasized the principles of 'non-interference in the internal affairs of States, and the non-use of human rights as an instrument of political pressure' and stressed the 'significance of national and regional particularities and various historical, cultural and religious backgrounds' to justify Vietnam's exception to the universal rule.

Although this was the first time that Vietnam used the 'Asian values' theory as a conceptual argument to challenge the West, the Vietnamese government has long held its own perception of human rights which differs markedly from the universal view. This paper seeks to examine both official and popular perceptions of human rights in Vietnam, the conflicting imperatives between the government's international human rights discourse and its internal repression of dissent, and the relevance of the Vietnamese cultural heritage especially Buddhism to the development of a contemporary, dynamic human rights culture in Vietnam.

Human Rights and Independence

The idea of human rights was introduced to Vietnam at the beginning of the twentieth century, initially by way of the French, who familiarized Vietnamese intellectuals with the works of Voltaire, Montesquieu, Jean Jacques Rousseau and the 1789 Declaration of the Rights of Man, and later through translations of Western thinking published in China and Japan. Perceived as a means of emancipating the individual, human rights became a central theme in the Vietnamese movement for independence from French colonial rule in the decades of the 1910s and 1920s. The first Vietnamese intellectuals to seriously examine this concept were Phan Boi Chau and Phan Chu Trinh, both of whom advocated 'the right to life, freedom and human rights for the Vietnamese people', although they differed on the methods by which this should be achieved. Phan Chu Trinh adopted a non-violent, legalist position, contending that non-violent advocacy within French colonial structures could bring about human rights through a process of education and reform. Phan Boi Chau chose the path of resistance, firmly convinced that human rights could never be achieved under the French colonialists' obscurantist policies which reduced the Vietnamese people to a state where they 'have ears but are forbidden to hear, have eyes but are forbidden to see, have arms and legs but are forbidden to move, have minds but are forbidden to think.' His vision of human rights was universal, and he believed that one day 'Human Rights will rise like a golden sun, flooding the world with light'.

Inspired by this example, many Vietnamese patriots adopted the human rights discourse in the 1930s to denounce political repression under the colonial regime. Articles calling for civil and political rights such as press freedom, worker rights and the right to set up trade unions were published in independent newspapers such as *Tieng Dan* [*The People's Voice*], *Tiêng ChuongRe* [*The Cracked Bell*], *Dân Chung* [*The People*] in central and southern Vietnam. A particularly forceful petition denouncing inhuman detention conditions in Vietnam and calling for the release of political prisoners was addressed to the French Overseas Territories' Inquiry Commission by a prominent revolutionary figure, Huynh Thuc Khang in 1937.

The Vietnamese Communists also adopted the discourse of human rights during this period, but primarily as a weapon to attack the French colonialists or to attract popular support to the international communist cause. Their prime objective was the establishment of a communist state, as can be seen by the peasants' demonstrations in Nghe An and Ha Tinh provinces in 1930-1931 which were portrayed as the 'Nghe Tinh Soviets'. Ideologically, the Vietnamese Communists rejected the idea that human rights belong to all people on the basis of human nature. They believed that rights were contingent on the class background, political opinions and revolutionary contribution of each individual, and that they reflected the objective economic and social conditions of each society. As Marxists, they considered civil and political rights as 'bourgeois'. As pragmatists, they perceived human rights in general as cumbersome impediments to their political goals. The people's ultimate right, in the Vietnamese Communists' view, was the right to national independence. Consequently, the establishment of an independent Communist state became synonymous with the fulfilment of human rights.

This concept is enshrined in Ho Chi Minh's 'Declaration of Independence' of the Democratic Republic of Vietnam pronounced on 2 September, 1945 which opens with the phrase from the 1776 American Declaration of Independence 'All men are created equal.' and continues: 'if we enlarge the sphere of our thoughts this statement conveys another meaning: All peoples on the earth are equal from birth, all peoples have the right to live, to be happy and free'. An article in the official *Tap Chi Công San* on 'The Declaration of Independence and the problem of Human Rights' analyses the key importance of this statement in the Vietnamese Communists' perspective:

By 'enlarging the sphere of thought' in such an original way, Ho Chi Minh established a totally logical and fitting link between individual rights and the rights of all peoples. Since individual rights are self-evident and natural, thence peoples' rights are also natural. From there, He [*sic*] concluded that all imperialist forces aggressing or encroaching upon Vietnam are acting against nature and violating human rights as defined by the American Declaration of Independence and the French Declaration of the Rights of Man. In regards to Vietnam, by establishing the parity between individual rights and peoples' rights as an irrefutable truth, Ho Chi Minh made an even more positive affirmation: that the creation of the Democratic Republic of Vietnam is self-evident and natural, for it emerges from the principles of human rights, and is approved of by history.

Thus, the core of the Vietnamese Communists' human rights concept consists of the belief that the establishment of the Democratic Republic of Vietnam (now the Socialist Republic of Vietnam [SRV], since re-unification with the South), under the leadership of the Vietnamese Communist Party (VCP) is in itself the fulfilment of individual human rights. Consequently, all those who are at odds with the Communist State are violating the people's rights. This is the key argument for the legitimacy of VCP rule, and it justifies measures to suppress criticism and maintain the VCP in power at all costs.

This concept is also reflected in the SRV's legal framework. Although four different Constitutions have been adopted since 1946 incorporating various guarantees in the domain of human rights, the official legal journal *Luat Hoc* (*Jurisprudence*) commented that 'each constitution ... is but the incarnation of the Party line and policies in a specific historical period, satisfies the needs of that stage, and must be suitable for the latter'.

Human Rights 'Debate' in Vietnam

Once Vietnam was united as the Socialist Republic of Vietnam on 2 July, 1976 there was no 'debate' on human rights, in the sense of an exchange of ideas. Official discussion was no longer necessary, the VCP considering that the Vietnamese people were now free from oppression and had thus achieved their basic rights. Unofficial discussion was prohibited. In North Vietnam, virtually all discussion of rights was silenced during the post-1954 period with the repression of the Nhan Van Giai Pham (Humanism Belles Letters), a movement for freedom of expression led by prominent writers and artists which, although similar to the Chinese 'Hundred Flowers' movement, was a spontaneous initiative on the part of writers and intellectuals, not a campaign orchestrated by the Party like its Chinese counterpart. Debate within the Communist Party itself was further curtailed in Vietnam in the 1960s, with the arrest of hundreds of Communist Party members accused of 'revisionism', including several generals, colonels and top-ranking officers from the People's Army, deputy ministers, editors of major official newspapers and even Ho Chi Minh's personal secretary, Vu Dinh Huynh. Some of these men, like Hoang Minh Chinh, former head of the Hanoi Institute of Marxist-Leninist Philosophy, were to spend the next 20 years in prison and under house arrest for questioning the orthodox Party line.

Human rights were taboo in the official media, raised exclusively as a measure of rhetorical self-defence in reaction to international pressure or domestic unrest. These sporadic official pronouncements nevertheless give an insight into the Vietnamese leaders' position on human rights. On 26 February 1978, during an official visit to New Delhi, SRV Prime Minister Pham Van Dong clearly articulated his Government's view that the right to national independence took precedence over all other human rights considerations a concept that Vietnam's leaders had never revealed to public opinion during the Vietnam war. Again, in 1979, in an attempt to defuse international outcry over the plight of Vietnamese boat people notably the campaign launched by the Vietnam Committee on Human Rights in Paris with the support of French intellectuals such as Jean-Paul Sartre and Raymond Aron to charter a 'Boat for Vietnam' VCP spokesman Nguyen Khac Vien coined the expression 'economic refugees' to justify this tragic exodus in which a million Vietnamese boat people perished on the South China Seas. But perhaps the most explicit and revealing official statement on human rights was the startling booklet entitled ' *Vietnam: What human rights?*' published by Hanoi's Foreign Language Publishing House in 1980. Designed to provide a response to international criticisms of the detention and ill-treatment of dissidents in notorious 're-education' camps in Vietnam, this booklet contained several articles which, as well as rebuffing foreign interference into internal Vietnamese affairs, argued that re-education was a clairvoyant and 'humane' policy. One article on 'Re-education Camps and Human Rights' even justified the practice of detention without trial: 'Re-education, not punishment this is the fundamental difference between our system and that of other countries, where incriminated people are brought up before courts of law. By dispensing people from a court sentence, our system spares them from having a criminal record which would affect their whole lives, and could even have repercussions on their children.' Fortunately, in this particular case, the force of international pressure had positive results, for Vietnam later abandoned *de jure* legislation on indefinite detention for re-education although *de facto*, many untried prisoners of conscience remain in jail.

New human rights language was incorporated into the official discourse during the late 1980s, when Vietnam embarked on its transition towards a 'Socialist-orientated market economy' and revised aspects of its legal framework. The revised Criminal Code and Criminal Procedures Code (1989) incorporated new guarantees such as the right to presumed innocence and the compensation of victims. Nevertheless, far from providing increased human rights protection, the new legislation presented a real set-back to human rights, codifying the suppression of political and religious dissent under a whole chapter of 'national security' offences, many of which are punishable with the death penalty. With the introduction of the new Criminal Code, prisoners of conscience became common criminals, thus enabling Vietnam to declare before the UN Human Rights Commission in Geneva that 'there are no political prisoners in Vietnam'.

However, at the same time that the government adopted the language of human rights, it continued unabatedly to violate human rights in Vietnam. Modelling its policy on that of China, Vietnam has adhered to a discourse of double standards, combining human rights dialogue abroad with a policy of repression at home. Whilst expanding contacts with Western countries, participating in exchange programmes and inviting foreign delegations to visit the country, Vietnam has stepped up political controls on freedom of opinion and expression, introducing legislation such as Decree 31/CP on 'Administrative Detention' adopted in 1997 which gives Security Police extrajudicial powers to arrest and detain any citizens suspected of 'threatening national security' for up to two years without a court order. In a climate of increasing restrictions and control, the government has continued to imprison dissidents and stifle all moves towards a human rights dialogue. In the official media, all form of debate remains completely one-sided, dominated by the regime which maintains a strict monopoly on the circulation of information and ideas.

Unofficial Movements for Human Rights

Of all the dissident movements in Vietnam, it was most of all the Buddhists, monks, nuns and lay-Buddhists of the independent Unified Buddhist Church (UBCV), who were the first to take up the language of human rights and inspire other movements to follow in their wake. The very first dissidents in the post-1975 era were twelve Buddhist monks and nuns who immolated themselves at Duoc Su Pagoda in Can Tho on 2 November, 1975 to protest against violations of religious freedom and human rights. In 1982, after the UBCV was officially banned, many prominent Buddhists were arrested and sentenced to long prison terms; two eminent scholars, Prof. Thich Tue Sy and Dr Le Manh That, were condemned to death in 1988 (their sentences were later commuted to 20 years hard labour due to international pressure). The UBCV Patriarch, Thich Huyen Quang and his Deputy Thich Quang Do were both sent into internal exile and placed under house arrest in 1982.

Following the demise of Communism in the Soviet Union and Eastern Europe, a new wave of democratic activism broke out in 1989-1992. Dr Nguyen Dan Que founded the 'Non-violent Movement for Human Rights', Prof. Doan Viet Hoat and a group of activists circulated a modest bulletin with news on the democratic struggle,

> *The Freedom Forum. At the same time, prominent South Vietnamese Communist Party veterans, revolutionary figures and several Generals and other top-ranking People's Army officers including Nguyen Ho, Ta Ba Tong, Nguyen Van Tran, La Van Liem and Lê Gian, formed 'The Club of Former Resistance Fighters' a movement which strongly criticized Party policies in its newspaper The Tradition of Resistance. In the North, liberal*

> *intellectuals and academics such as Phan Dinh Dieu and Ha Si Phu circulated essays calling for democratic freedoms and political reform. These appeals were indiscriminately silenced. The establishment critics escaped with relatively 'discrete' sanctions — Phan Dinh Dieu lost his job as Deputy Director of the National Centre of Scientific Research but the Club of Former Resistance Fighters was disbanded, its newspaper banned and its leaders arrested. Doan Viet Hoat and Nguyen Dan Que received harsh prison sentences of 15 and 20 years respectively.*

The suppression of these unofficial movements for free expression and press freedom sparked off heated protests, especially amongst critics close to the Communist Party who had genuinely hoped that the VCP would take the initiative to instigate democratic reforms. In a petition to the Party written shortly before his arrest, Nguyen Ho, President of the Club of Former Resistance Fighters, a veteran labour leader and Party member for 60 years, wrote:

> *I find it so hard to understand why, when the South (Cochinchina) was under colonial rule, Communists took advantage of the right to freedom of the press guaranteed in the metropolis (Imperialist France) to publish independent newspapers such as comrade Nguyen Van Nguyen's L'Avant-garde (Tiên Phong) or Nguyen Van Tran's Le Peuple (Dân Chung) in 1938. They didn't even have to apply for a permit, they just sent off a 'simple déclaration'. Whereas today, under the Socialist regime the regime of freedom former resistance fighters are not allowed to publish their own newspaper or even write articles, despite the fact that freedom of the press is guaranteed by the Constitution as one of the citizens' fundamental rights.*

After his release from house arrest, Nguyên Hô pushed his criticisms even further in a 50-page type-written booklet entitled *Quan Diêm và Cuôc Sông* [*View-point and Daily Life*] circulated unofficially in Vietnam. He charged the Party not only of betraying the people by violating human rights, but also of betraying the international community by acceding to human rights instruments such as the UN Universal Declaration of Human Rights, then blatantly violating this pledge. Worse still, he wrote, was the 'reign of terror' subsisting in Communist Vietnam:

> The Party always claims to be the vanguard in the people's movement for liberation, but throughout the decades it has been in power, the Party has dispossessed the people of their fundamental freedoms and democratic rights, plunging them in the darkest ignorance. From there, the Party has imposed a reign of terror all over the country, striking fear of the Party even into the hearts of veteran officials and cadres. The whole population lives in terror of the Party, exactly as they lived in terror of the emperors and feudal rulers of yore. This is why many people remain silent in face of the Party's mistakes. They dare not express their opinions because they are too afraid. This is the most devastating and harmful consequence of the totalitarian dictatorship in place in Vietnam today.

Democracy, he stressed, is aspired to by all people. It is not the exclusive right of the English, the Americans or the French. The Party is denouncing Western concepts of democracy and freedom as a pretext to suppress the freedoms of its own people. Nguyên Hô challenged the Party to recognize its errors and take steps to put things right.

Other South Vietnamese Communist veterans such as Nguyên Van Trân , quoted in Nguyên Hô's Petition, echoed these protests in a monumental book of memoirs, *Viêt cho Me và Quôc Hôi* [*Written for my Mother and the National Assembly*] which was published privately by the author in Ho Chi Minh City in 1995 and immediately banned by the authorities. Looking back at his years of struggle, Nguyên Van Trân stressed the crucial importance of press freedom as the basis of all human rights: 'I can only say this: today, as in 1938, I devote myself to the struggle for freedom of the press, using freedom of expression as a thorn to prize out the thorns of human rights abuses embedded in society's flesh'.

Unofficial discussion of human rights was silenced

briefly after 1995 following the arrest of virtually all the Buddhist leadership, as well as a number of critics close to the Communist Party, e.g. Do Trung Hieu, Le Hong Ha, Hoang Minh Chinh and Ha Si Phu. But discontent remained widespread in Vietnam, and in 1997 protests erupted all over the country, notably in the northern province of Thai Binh and the predominantly Catholic districts of Dong Nai in the south, where scores of thousands of peasants demonstrated against corruption, official power abuse and the confiscation of land. Criticisms are also being voiced with increasing insistence today by liberal intellectuals and veterans of the VCP who are pressing the Party's new leadership to become the spearhead for change. In a series of extremely forthright statements and letters to the Vietnamese authorities issued in December 1997 January 1998, General Trân Dô, former Deputy Minister of Culture and Deputy Head of the Communist Party's Department of Propaganda, Phan Dinh Dieu, mathematician and former Head of the Information Institute, Hoang Minh Chinh, former Chancellor of the Institute of Marxist-Leninist Philosophy, geophysicist Nguyen Thanh Giang and a number of other former VCP officials wrote to the Vietnamese authorities warning that the Communist Party faced 'collapse' unless it made immediate, radical reforms. In a speech delivered to the Expanded Presidium of the Fatherland Front on 13 December 1997, Phan Dinh Dieu emphasized:

> *The need for democracy in the political realm has become imperative. New ideas and thinking which are opposite to the Party's orthodox line have all been prohibited. The modernisation of society requires fundamental democratic rights such as freedom of thought, freedom of expression, freedom of the press, freedom of association, freedom to vote and to run for office.*

This speech is noteworthy, not only because of its rights-based content, but also because it was delivered before a Party Committee. It thus approaches what might be termed a 'debate' between the Party and the critics. However, as these lines are being written, dozens of threatening articles have appeared in the official media attacking 'individuals who abuse human rights to undermine national security', so there is little cause for optimism as yet.

It is important to stress, moreover, that although these statements, letters and speeches have been widely circulated and debated within the Vietnamese community overseas, thanks to smuggled copies and translations relayed on the Internet, they remain strictly prohibited in Vietnam. Not only are such texts forbidden in the official media most people would not have heard of them without outside news sources such as the BBC, VOA, Radio France Internationale or Radio Free Asia but all persons found in possession of such documents, including the authors themselves, risk sanctions and arrest. In a letter to the National Assembly (26 March 1998) geophysicist Nguyen Thanh Giang describes how he was arrested and interrogated for several days after Security Police caught him with an article he wrote on General Tran Do copies of which he had sent to VCP Party Secretary Lê Kha Phiêu and several members of the Politburo over a month before. General Trân Dô himself protested in a letter to National Assembly President Nong Duc Manh on 20 April, 1998 that his daughter-in-law had been subjected to several weeks of intense police interrogations because she was found with copies of his writings and a book of banned poetry, *Spontaneous Poetry from the Interrogation Room, by another Government critic, Bui Minh Quoc.*

'Vietnam Values': The Official View

Vietnam entered a new phase of the human rights 'debate' in 1993, when for the very first time, literally hundreds of articles on human rights were published in the official media. This unprecedented output was triggered off by two major events. The first was the UN World Conference on Human Rights in Vienna and its Preparatory Regional Meeting in

Bangkok where Vietnam first adhered to the Asian values premise. The second was a demonstration of 40,000 Buddhists in the ancient capital of Hue on 24 May, 1993. This massive public protest the first of its kind in Communist Vietnam shook the authorities deeply, for they were totally unprepared for a popular challenge of such proportions.

The debate in the official media was divided into two categories of articles: (a) theoretical analysis of the human rights premise in an attempt to elaborate a concept based on 'Vietnamese values', and (b) caustic attacks on the Buddhist demonstrators in Hue for 'abusing human rights and religion to harm the interests of the State'. Ironically, these articles merely served to highlight the contradictions in Vietnam's cultural relativist argument, since the very same 'Vietnamese values' advanced in the former category were strongly criticized in the latter. One essay on ' Human Rights and Vietnamese Ethics', incorporated both conflicting views. Arguing in favour of a Vietnamese human rights concept based on the Buddhist principles of tolerance and compassion, it cited the example of fifteenth-century King Lê Loi and his Buddhist statesman Nguyên Trai who, after defeating the Chinese in battle, ordered boats to be built to transport the Chinese prisoners of war back home. Yet it ended with a sombre condemnation of Buddhism in Vietnam, denouncing all those who 'hide under the cloak of religion' to oppose the Party and the State, and equating Buddhist activism with 'peaceful evolution', a global conspiracy waged by 'hostile forces' to undermine the regime. This contradictory position characterizes the official attitude even today. Whereas Vietnam's officials and academics praise the political engagement of Buddhist emperors and statesmen in the Ly and Tran dynasties, they condemn and imprison modern-day Buddhists who merely voice appeals for a minimal respect of religious freedom and human rights.

This was the first and last time 'Vietnamese values' were alluded to in the official press. The media campaign was followed by a widespread crackdown on the Buddhists, and prominent clergy and lay-followers were arrested in its wake. It was also the first and the last time that the authorities experimented with television to put their message across. In what was something of a premiere in Communist Vietnam, footage of the Hue demonstration had been shown on national television in order to portray an 'extremist' image of the monks. However, this strategy seriously backfired, only attracting increased public sympathy to the Buddhist cause.

After 1993, human rights once again became a taboo in the State controlled media. Again faithful to the Chinese example, Vietnam withdrew to the 'non-interference' stance, raising human rights only in highly polemic statements to rebuff interference by Western governments and international NGOs. Vietnam had perhaps realized that the 'Asian values' issue was a real Pandora's box, which, if opened, could unleash popular currents and forces beyond the scope of Government control.

Foundations of True 'Vietnamese Values

Although I find no foundation in Vietnam's theory of cultural exceptionalism, I do believe that Vietnam has its own traditional and original concept of human rights based more on ethics than on law which reinforces, rather than detracts, from the universal rule. Indeed, individual rights and freedoms are a fundamental and ancient feature of Vietnamese culture, rooted in a cultural heritage over four thousand years old. The two pillars of this concept are Buddhism, which reached Vietnam more than 20 centuries ago, and Confucianism, which the Buddhists integrated into the State apparatus from the eleventh century onwards.

Confucianism has many different schools, but all are united in the belief that the universe is governed by three driving forces Heaven, Earth and Humankind and that Humankind is the central pivot of all. As Mencius (ca. 380-289 BC) said, 'The people are of paramount importance, second comes the State and last comes the Sovereign, who is least important of all'. On a similar basis to the 'Western' concept of human rights, Confucianism recognizes the legitimate right to resist oppression, and to overthrow the ruler if he is unjust. To use the image of Xunzi (ca. 340-305 BC), 'Water can keep the boat afloat, but can also overturn it'.

But it is undoubtedly Buddhism, introduced into Vietnam from India in the first century AD, and adhered to by three-quarters of the population in Vietnam today, which inspired the culture of liberty, social justice and tolerance inherent in Vietnamese traditions, and made the most important contribution to the development of Vietnamese civilization and the foundation of an independent political system in Vietnam.

The Buddhist concept of human rights dates back 2,500 years, when Sakyamuni Buddha revolutionized the thinking of his time by defying the caste system and demanding the integration of pariahs (untouchables) and women into the clergy, thus becoming one of the world's first advocates of equality and gender rights: 'There can be no caste system, no discrimination between beings whose blood is identically red, and whose every drop of sweat is tinged with salt'. Although Buddhism does not enshrine individualism as it is perceived in the West, but rather 'Vo Nga', the Non-self, or interdependence, there is perhaps no higher tribute to the inherent dignity, equality and inalienable rights of the individual than that expressed by Sakyamuni Buddha when he declared, 25 centuries before the UN Declaration of Human Rights: 'Each person is the Buddha to be'. This means that every individual is endowed with buddhahood, the potential ability to extinguish suffering and injustice for the liberation of humankind, and with the capacity to overcome every imaginable form of slavery, oppression and ignorance. Thus, the Buddhist vision of human rights, based on the mutually reinforcing precepts of Karuna (compassion, love) and Prajna (absolute knowledge), not only defines the framework for the protection of human rights, but re-examines the whole question of mankind's place at the centre of society and within the universe.

Vietnamese Buddhism is deeply impregnated with this spirit of freedom and social justice; in fact it was the influence of Buddhism that ensured the survival of Vietnamese civilization and formed the basis of Vietnamese cultural identity. Whereas all the other 'Bach Viet' (Hundred Viet) tribes from the provinces of Guangdong and Guangxi were absorbed by China, only the Viet people in Giao Châu (modern day Vietnam) survived, preserving a unity of thinking, language and culture from the origins of their history until today. The profound influence of Buddhism on Vietnamese thinking and cultural expression also stems from the fact that Buddhism was introduced into Vietnam through the oral narration of Buddhist '*Jataka*', simple tales of the Buddha's earlier lives, rather than through learned Buddhist sutras accessible only to the intelligentsia. Thus, Buddhist thinking permeated Vietnamese society from the grass-roots upwards, rather than being imposed from above.

Besides its profound impact on the people's development in the spiritual realm, in the social and historical realms Vietnamese Buddhism developed from the very outset a tradition of activism and a commitment to social justice unique in South East Asia. Predominantly following the Mahayana school, which stresses the link between self-enlightenment and the commitment to emancipate one's fellows from ignorance and injustice, Vietnamese Buddhists practice 'engaged Buddhism', actively participating in all aspects of the nation's social and political life. Early Vietnamese Buddhist sutras such as the *Luc Dô Tâp Kinh* [*Book of Six Ways of Liberation*] dating back to the second century AD taught these principles of individual engagement: '[Each one must say to him/herself], if the people are unhappy, it is my own fault', or 'When the Boddhisattva hears the cries of his people, he must set aside his own troubles and throw himself into the combat against tyranny, whereby saving the people from suffering'. The sutra also articulated the Buddhist vision of an ideal society which defines extremely modern concepts such as the protection of the environment, social equality, promotion of universal education, the practice of non-violence and clemency in all affairs of State.

The Buddhist spirit of liberation defined in these early sutras encompasses the combat against obscurantism (liberation from ignorance), the combat for social justice (liberation from suffering) and the struggle for national independence (liberation from foreign oppression), in brief, the liberation of the individual, the community and the nation. Inspired with this spirit, the Vietnamese raised innumerable resistance armies to free their homeland from Chinese domination over more than nine centuries. Their armies counted scores of thousand men an astounding achievement for a population estimated at 981,735 in the second century AD. Moreover, the Buddhist concept of equality and social justice permeated all organizational levels of the State, to an extent that took the Chinese invaders by surprise. Mouzi, a Chinese Taoist and Confucianist who came to Giao Châu (Vietnam) in the late second century was so impressed by Vietnamese civilization that he became a Buddhist and in 198 AD wrote the *Ly Hoac Luan* [*Doubts Raised*], a 37-chapter critique of Chinese Confucianist and Taoist ethics in which he exclaimed: 'Perhaps the Han nation is not the centre of the universe after all!' Moreover, the annals of Chinese history relate that in 43 AD, when China invaded Vietnam, the Vietnamese already had an advanced legal system which 'differed in ten points from the system of Chinese law'.

Throughout the whole period of Chinese domination, Zen Buddhist monks played a prominent role in resistance movements and contributed largely to the foundation of the first independent Vietnamese State in the tenth century AD. In the eleventh and thirteenth centuries, Buddhist monarchs of the Ly and Tran dynasties heralded a golden age in which politics, culture, diplomacy, science and the arts flourished as never before. Under the Lê dynasty in the fifteenth century, the outstanding Hong Duc Penal Code was drawn up which codified modern concepts in advance of contemporary European equivalents:

We see in Lê Dynasty... a peculiarly Vietnamese effort at building a strong nation-state and protecting legitimate private rights through a progressive legal system with many functional equivalents to contemporary Western legal concepts. We see in Lê law a rather modern legal order, in which there were notions and practices equivalent to present-day Western legal standards, such as the protection of civil liability compensation (including punitive damages) for the victims and the guarantees of procedural due process for the defendants in criminal law, the larger role of public policy in favour of the economically weak in contract law, the consistent and explicit provision of damages payments for all kinds of torts against property, person and reputation, the fair distribution and protection of property ownership, the equality of men and women in civil and property rights, and last but not least, the popularization and standardization of legal forms used among the population.

The Buddhist spirit of liberation was also the driving force of the Vietnamese independence movement against French colonialist rule. An important Buddhist 'Renaissance' movement in the 1920s to 1930s launched vast educational programmes to counteract the colonialists' obscurantist policies, and although Buddhists sought no political role, monks, nuns and followers participated actively in national resistance movements after 1945. Subsequently, although Buddhism was virtually suppressed in North Vietnam under the government of Ho Chi Minh, it continued to exercise an important influence in the South, especially after the overthrow of the Ngo Dinh Diem regime in 1963, stimulating the country's cultural, social and educational life through a whole network of nursery, primary and secondary schools, Institutes of Advanced Buddhist studies, and prestigious avant-garde universities such as Van Hanh University in Saigon which taught humanities, social sciences and modern languages to over 5,000 students. The Buddhists' independent stance was especially salient during the Vietnam war, when UBCV monks massively opposed war and campaigned for a peace solution that would win political independence for Vietnam and preserve the country from becoming a satellite of either the socialist or capitalist blocs.

Role of Buddhism in Modern Society

Buddhism in Vietnam does not have well-established, structured institutions comparable to religions in the West, in part because of its philosophy of harmony and tolerance, which enables Buddhism to co-exist peacefully without seeking to impose on other religious or political creeds, but also because it has never enjoyed a time of peace to build and consolidate. Because it has remained independent of political control, supporting the State in times of need, checking its powers when the State became too authoritarian or corrupt, Vietnamese Buddhism has been the constant target of repression from a succession of regimes, from feudal to colonial, from militarist to communist. It is therefore impossible to pinpoint Buddhism to a particular social category, or isolate its sphere of influence to a particular sector of political life. But it is clear that Buddhism by which I mean the independent Unified Buddhist Church, not the State-controlled Vietnam Buddhist Church set up by the Communist authorities in 1981 is playing a crucial role in Vietnamese society today, despite prohibitive government repression. Its impact can be seen in two specific domains: the dynamic and pervasive influence of Buddhist thinking throughout all levels of society, and especially its impact on the Marxist intelligentsia; and the role of the UBCV as the driving force of the movement for human rights and democracy in Vietnam.

Throughout the 1990s, the influence of Buddhist thinking on Marxist intellectuals has become remarkably clear. Before 1975, studies by Hanoi's most eminent historians and ethnologists revealed the paucity of their research material and their total lack of understanding of Buddhism, the consequence of decades of anti-religious policies and the draconian suppression of non-Marxist literature in North Vietnam. Today, however, Marxist intellectuals are beginning to have wider access through official and underground channels to books published in the South, particularly works written in 1963-1975, a period when Zen literature flourished, stimulating bold currents of creation and research amongst a whole generation of Buddhist and non-Buddhist writers alike. Eminent Marxist scholars such as Ha Van Tan are beginning to re-evaluate their historical research in the light of these new perspectives, familiarize themselves with Buddhist humanist concepts and make a reappraisal of Buddhism's historical role in the foundation of the Vietnamese civilization and State. In the long term, this suffusion of Buddhist thinking into Marxist dogma will have indelible effects on the political perceptions of future generations in Vietnam.

In the practical domain, Buddhism has emerged as the only popular force consistently struggling for the defence of human rights in Vietnam. At every level, from democratic activism on a national scale to engagement in local community affairs, UBCV monks, nuns and lay followers are actively engaged in efforts for social justice, denouncing violations wherever they occur. The most eloquent articulation of the UBCV human rights position and one that unleashed a wave of Government repression against the Buddhists is the 'Declaration' issued in 1993 by the UBCV's Supreme Patriarch, Thich Huyen Quang. In this, he called for radical democratic reforms, the right to political pluralism and free elections under UN supervision and stressed the decisive role of religious communities in Vietnam's democratic process:

After 50 years of devastating war waged in the name of conflicting, imported ideologies, religious movements alone possess an unparalleled capacity to temper hatreds, defuse conflict and restore moral values in a society plunged in a spiritual and moral crisis. As such, they have a vital role to play in the reconstruction of our country.

The key to democracy is tolerance, wrote Thich Huyen Quang, and tolerance lies in the hands of the State. Democratic freedoms and human rights cannot exist, either in principle or in practice, until Vietnam abolishes Article 4 of its Constitution regarding the monopoly of the Communist Party:

The abolition of Article 4 does not imply the exclusion or the dissolution of the Communist Party. It will stimulate the participation of all sectors of the population, regardless of their political affiliations or religious beliefs [and] foster competition as a mutually reinforcing relationship, not as a race to oust one's opponents. After all, whether our compatriots be communists or members of any other political party, they are first and foremost Vietnamese. Our common heritage of 5,000 years' civilization will form the basis for future dialogue and co operation, and we will be bound together in one common aim that of forging a place within the community of nations for a stable, flourishing and prosperous Vietnam.

This 'Declaration', written from the Patriarch's place of exile in Quang Ngai where he has been detained under house arrest since 1982, inspired human rights activists in Vietnam and emboldened them to openly express dissent. The massive Buddhist demonstration which broke out in Hue in 1993 set an example that would later be followed by peasants in Thai Binh and Nam Dinh and by Catholics in Dong Nai, indicating a growing popular awareness of human rights.

Paradox of the 'Asian Values' Premise in Vietnam

Whereas the Buddhist vision of human rights is genuinely universal, seeking the liberation of Asian societies from authoritarian, militarist and totalitarian rule and the establishment of a new human rights culture for the twenty-first century, the Communist authorities are turning back the clock. Just as French colonialists relied on alcohol, opium, and superstition to maintain the people in ignorance, Vietnam is now reviving antiquated rites, festivals and folklore to assuage the people's spiritual needs and to maintain political control. At the same time, it is developing State-sponsored religious bodies whose activities are strictly confined to the celebration of prayers, meditation, fasting, even fortune telling, thus supplanting freedom of religion with the minimal right to freedom of worship and reducing religion to the practice of quasi-superstitious rites.

The long-term implications of this policy are extremely serious, and they lie at the core of the current discussion on Asian values in Vietnam. By emptying the great religions of their moral and spiritual content and preventing them from contributing their immense potential to the development of a vibrant, stable and prosperous society in Vietnam, Vietnam is stifling civil society and jeopardizing the country's future for generations to come.

If there is any significance in the Asian values debate, it is the reminder that the dynamic, humanist values inherent in the cultures of Vietnam, China, Tibet, Burma, Indonesia and other Asian countries are threatened today not by 'Western imposed' human rights concepts, but by the practices and policies of their very own governments who are using this argument to suppress these values and violate human rights with impunity.

5

Human Rights and Dignity in Communities

Introduction

Human rights are a modern concept now universally applicable in principle because of the social evolution of the entire world toward state societies. The concept of human rights springs from modern human thought about the nature of just; it does not spring from an anthropologically based consensus about the values, needs, or desires of human beings. As Jack Donnelly puts it, the concept of human rights is best interpreted by constructivist theory:

Human rights aim to establish and guarantee the conditions necessary for the development of the human person envisioned in underlying moral theory of human nature, thereby bringing into being that type of person. The evolution of particular conceptions or lists of human rights is seen in the constructivist theory as the result of the *reciprocal interactions of moral conceptions and material conditions of life*, mediated through social institutions such as rights.

Human rights tend to be particularly characteristic of liberal and/or social democratic societies. These are societies that have undergone changes in the material conditions of life, or, in Marxist terms, in the mode of production, in the direction of various forms of capitalism. These material changes coincided with various changes in ideology or moral conceptions, both in the strictly religious sphere and in conceptions of how society ought to be organized and of what makes a physical human being a social being. Ideologically rights-based societies, then, hold particular conceptions of human dignity and social justice that are in principle universally applicable, although not universal in origin. While ideals of dignity and justice can be located in all societies and can sometimes be used to buttress new ideals of the content of human rights, human rights are a radically new concept in human history, and their acceptance in any given society constitutes a rupture of previous belief systems.

Human Rights, Dignity and Justice

Human rights adhere to the human being *by virtue of being human, and for no other reason Every human being ought to have human rights, regardless of status or achievement.* In a rights-based political system, a person's human rights can in principle be removed only under very restricted circumstances adjudicable by law (for example, a convicted criminal loses the right to freedom of movement). Human rights *are claims by the individual against society and the state* that, furthermore, "trump" other considerations such as the legal (but not human) right of a corporation to property. Human rights are private, individual, and autonomous. They are private because they inhere in the human person him- or herself, unmediated by social relations. They are consequently individual; an isolated human being can in principle exercise them. In addition, they are autonomous because again, in principle, no authority other than the individual is required to make human rights claims.

This means that the human being who holds rights holds them not only against the state, but also against "society," that is, against his or her community or even family. This orientation is a radical departure from the way most human societies in the past and many in the present have been or are organized. For most human societies, insofar as "rights" might be considered to be applicable at all, collective or communal rights would be preferred to individual human rights. The stress on community as against the individual is reflected in the current debate in international legal circles over whether "human" rights should also include collective rights. But the claim for collective rights is a claim for something very different from human rights; it is a claim that reasserts the value of the traditional community over the individual. Human rights are an egalitarian means of allocating membership in a collectivity to all physical persons, regardless of status. Collective or community rights imply permissible inegalitarian ranking of members in the interests of preservation of "tradition."

Dignity

I define human dignity as *the particular cultural understandings of the inner moral worth of the human person and his or her proper political relations with society.* Dignity is not a claim that an individual asserts against a society; it is not, for example, the claim that one is worthy of respect merely because one is a human being. Rather, dignity is something that is granted at birth or on incorporation into the community as a concomitant of one's particular ascribed status, or that accumulates and is earned during the life of an adult who adheres to his or her society's values, customs, and norms: the adult, that is, who accepts normative cultural constraints on his or her particular behaviour. In many preliterate societies, individuals who chose not to earn such dignity, who consistently violated instead of obeying the underlying social norms, were cast out through exile or through conversion into slavery. As the sociologist Orlando Patterson explains, as slaves they lost all honour (or dignity) and suffered "natal alienation"; that is, they were literally cast out from their own family group and removed from the networks of privileges and obligations that tied society together.

Many indigenous groups (that is, the remnants of precapitalist societies destroyed physically, culturally, or both during the process of European conquest and/or settlement) now make claims for the recognition of their collective or communal rights. When they do so they are not primarily interested in the human rights of the individual members of their collectivities. Rather, they are interested in the recognition of their *collective dignity*, in the acknowledgment of the value of their collective way of life as opposed to the way of life of the dominant society into which they are unequally "integrated." In Canada, this means, among other things, the recognition of the land rights and the fishing, hunting, and trapping rights of collective First Nation or "Native" groups, so that they can maintain an agricultural or hunting and gathering mode of production despite the prevailing capitalism of the dominant European-origin society.

That these collective rights-claims are not synonymous with individual human rights is well illustrated by the recent debate and legislative changes in Canada concerning the right of Native women who married outside the reserves (and their descendants) to return to live on reserves. Some Native women claimed, and all were eventually granted, the right to move back onto reserves; they based their claim on the grounds of equality of women and men. But such grounds stem from the Enlightenment tradition of human rights incorporated in the twentieth century into such documents as the Universal Declaration of Human Rights. Counterposed against the Native women claiming their right of return were some Native leaders who argued for their collective right to determine who would live on a reserve, in such a manner as to preserve the integrity of the Native community even at the possible expense of individual women's rights. The issue was compounded by the fact that the rule expelling intermarried Native women was originally imposed by European-origin Canadians, who used their own patrilineal and patrilocal culture as a means of enforcing assimilation and reducing the number of Indians entitled to treaty rights. Thus Native Canadians, engaged in a continual struggle to preserve their collective dignity, were doubly at the mercy of changes in European ideologies of social membership. The conflict between concepts of individual human rights that require equality of the sexes, and collective rights to a group dignity that might countenance inequality of the sexes, remains.

Thus in most known past or present societies, human dignity is not private, individual, or autonomous. It is public, collective, and prescribed by social norms. The idea that an individual can enhance his or her "dignity" by asserting his or her human rights violates many societies' most fundamental beliefs about the way social life should be ordered. Part of the dignity of a human being consists of the quiet endurance and acceptance of what a human rights approach to the world would consider injustice or inequality. We can see this underlying social belief most clearly in modern North America in the reaction of many men and women to feminists. Women making rights-claims against the state, society, and the family are frequently depicted as "shrill," "strident," or overly emotional. Such depictions emphasize the undignified way in which they are behaving when they refuse to bear injustice as properly socialized women should. This brings us to the question, then, of what exactly "justice" means.

Justice

Different societies have different conceptions of social justice. I define social justice as *the means by which all members of a society are treated in a fashion considered respectful of their (culturally defined) social station.* Justice consists of rules of appropriate social behaviour and rules of fairness. Fairness, in most societies, does not imply equality either of wealth or of social status. What is fair varies according to whether one is young or old, male or female, "citizen" or stranger, chief, freeman, or slave; and within these summary categories, there are infinite gradations of status, such as can be seen in the caste system of India.

There are some medications of a cross-cultural, anthropologically based consensus of what fairness ought to entail. Barrington Moore, Jr., for example, suggests that in almost all societies, everyone is expected to work and there is a minimum level of subsistence that a working person can rightfully expect from the society at large. There are, he believes, "indications or a widespread feeling that people, even the most humble members of society, ought to have enough resources or facilities to do their job in the social order." But as his reference to the "most humble" member of society indicates, even if one is treated fairly, one is not necessarily treated equally. Status differences mean differences in dignity, in the respect to which one as entitled, and in the type of justice one can therefore expect.

In modern liberal-democratic societies, the idea of different laws for different categories of persons is anathema. All are subject to the same rules. But in many past societies, laws varied depending on one's social category, and such variation was considered "just" by the majority of citizens socialized into that society. Thus, for example, if a European lord exercised his *droit du seigneur* over a peasant woman (the right to have sexual intercourse with her prior to marriage), that was not considered rape, whereas a sexual advance by a peasant male to a noble's daughter risked a severe penalty. For the same crimes, lords received more humane punishments, for example, simple hangings than peasants, who might be tortured. Even clothing was regulated by sumptuary laws in order to ensure that everyone's social status was easily apparent. Until the

French Revolution, members of the French peasantry were not permitted to wear red; the "traditional" clothing of Breton peasants is in fact a modern adoption of red following the overthrow of Louis XVI.

Thus human rights imply a particular conception of what it means to be human. In the lexicon of human rights, humanity is a mere physical attribute; one is or is not a live human being. In most societies' lexicons of dignity and justice, however, to be human is a social attribute. There are degrees of humanity, the lowest being that of the slave, who is considered "socially dead."

For many societies, the human being is the person who has learned and obeys the community's rules. A nonsocial, atomized individual is not human; he or she is a species of "other" perhaps equivalent to a (presocialized) child, a stranger, a slave, or even an animal. There is very little room in most societies for Mead's "I" the individual, self-reflective being to emerge over the "me," that part of a being that aborbs his or her community's culture and faithfully follows the rules and customs expected of a person of his or her station. The human group takes precedence over the human person.

In Freudian terms, perhaps more familiar to most thinkers about human rights than the sociological analysis of what makes a physical human a social person, mary sociological suppress the ego. Individualist reflection on the meaning and personal applicability of the rules that the child absorbs into his or her superego is not socially desirable. The type of human being that liberal capitalist society has created frequently highly individualistic and self-seeking, alienated by choice from family and community is not valued. Rather, the motion of honor retains its importance, and the honored person is someone integrated into the social group: "honour is a direct expression of status, a source of solidarity among social equals and a declaration line against social inferiors." But in the modern world the "homeless mind" has displaced the concept of honour. The individual whose egoistic reflection causes him to modify his perceptions of the social order embodied in the superego, and who goes so far as to impose his own desires over that social order, denies honour; and in so doing, he denies society itself.

This does not mean that human rights are not relevant, in the late twentieth century, to those societies in the world that retain precapitalist, non-individualist notions of human dignity, honour, and the social order. The rise of the centralized state makes human rights relevant the world over. It does mean that to look for universalistic "roots" of human rights in different social areas of the world (often crudely summarized in geographical terms as "Africa" or "Asia") or in different religious traditions, is to abstract those societies and religions from culture and history. One can find, in Judaism and Christianity for example, strong moral analogues to the content although not the concept of contemporary human rights. But one can also find moral precepts justifying inequality and denial of what are now considered fundamental human rights. In the words of Arthur Schlesinger, Jr.:

> *As a historian, I confess to a certain amusement when I hear the Judeo Christian tradition praised as the source of our concern for human rights. In fact, the great religious ages were notable for their indifference to human rights in the contemporary sense. They were notorious not only for acquiescence in poverty, inequality, exploitation and oppression but for enthusiastic justifications of slavery, persecution, abandonment of small children, torture, genocide.*

Religion enshrined and vindicated hierarchy, authority and inequality.

In many nonlibeal societies (and among many members of liberal democratic polities), now and in the past, there are and have been very deeply rooted, perhaps psychologically inviolable, notions of moral order that obviate a belief in human equality and autonomy. In such societies, religious and community norms frequently entrench social inequalities that are considered immutable and reflective of the natural world. The status inequalities of human beings reflect notions of cosmological rectitude; violations of inequality, therefore, violate not only the human but also the natural order of things.

Order and Chaos

In primitive societies the imperative to create social order guards against the possibility of cosmological chaos. Identifications of men with the sun and women with the moon, men with the right hand and women with the left, men with cleanliness and women with dirt, and a host of other dichotomous interpretations of the obvious biological dichotomy of the human world, ensure that the sun will rise and set as it should, that the gods will not suddenly destroy all. Anomaly and ambiguity, as Mary Douglas has informed us, are shunned; in the marginal interstices between orderly categories danger lies:

> *Purity as the enemy of change, of ambiguity and compromise. Most of us feel safer if our experience is hard-set and fixed in form. The yearning for rigidity is in us all. It is part of our human condition to long for hard lines and clear concepts.*

The easiest and clearest social distinction to make is between men and women; in many societies, as our own language reflects, the male is the standard of humanness and the female is the deviation. As Simone de Beauvoir put it in her classic feminist meditation, to be female is to be the existential "Other." The female is the threat, in many cultures, to the orderliness created by males. Her body alone violates order; she bleeds though she is not wounded. The female possessed of knowledge threatens the orderly acquisition and delimitation of society's cognitive symbols created in most cultures by her male status superiors; thus from Eve to medieval wise-women and beyond, Judeo-Christian culture has punished the woman who exercises the *human* capacity for self-reflection with its attendant threat of making claims upon society.

Morality and Deviance

Most societies, then, are rule-bound. Violations not only of law but also of custom are severely sanctioned. Far from religion's having normally validated what are now considered to be human rights, religious authorities in the past made it their business to reinforce status inequalities and punish transgressors of social customs. In early modern Britain, priests could still sentence social deviants such as adulterers to ostracism and the stocks. In 1785 the Scottish poet Robert Burns did public penance in church for the sin of fornication (after which he was released from his marriage vows). Persons not publicly punished for moral transgressions could be shunned, ostracized, or exiled on the orders of religious or community authorities.

Such punishments seem strange to modern eyes. In modern Western society, the power of the priest to sentence his parishioners to shunning, ostracism, and expulsion from the community is difficult to understand. Most individuals in our society interact simultaneously with a multiplicity of communities. Family, friends, work associates, and religious co-believers may have nothing to do with each other and may be completely compartmentalized aspects of an individual's social life; thus a shunning ordered by a priest would not be effective. Only in almost completely closed social groups, such as those of the Amish in the United States or the Hutterites in Canada, can the power of shunning still be effective.

Rule-bounded societies exact punishments for non-conformity that violate fundamental human rights. Torture, a practice universally abhorred by those who favour human rights, is not, as frequently stated, a "cruel, *inhuman* and degrading" treatment. Cruel it certainly is, degrading it is frequently meant to be: inhuman it is not. The human body is a symbol for the entire moral and natural universe. The being who violates the moral universe is corrected by having his or her physical universe violated in turn. Submission or the body to social punishment indicates conformity of the mind: that is, acceptance of the social order and one's place in it.

In such closed traditional societies, maintenance of one's dignity or honour is frequently more important than one's individual "rights," even to life. Dishonour freely sought was severely sanctioned in earlier times. Thus the female rape victim in early Hammaburati society was assumed to have been complicitous in any rape committed within the city walls (where her cries for help should have been heard), and was punished accordingly. "Death before dishonour" was the cry of an earlier world, where a woman's purity was her greatest symbolic attribute; nowadays, the modern North American woman considers such a slogan merely an indication of the degraded status of women. "Dignified" victims of rape are no longer expected to commit suicide or to seclude themselves in shame for the rest of their lives.

Like torture, capital punishment also upholds the moral order. In liberal societies of the present time, the morality of capital punishment is a subject for serious debate, and indeed in Canada and in the European Community it is no longer practiced. Many theorists of criminology deny the moral legitimacy of punishment, advocating that prisons be places of rehabilitation or, at worst, simple deterrence of future crimes. In most societies, however, retribution is the explicit principle that decrees how criminals are to be treated. Executions are public because they thereby demonstrate to those who obey the law the rectitude of their own actions, in comparison to those of the victims of the executioner's sword. The function of punishment is confirmation of social norms. Thus even in France of Revolutionary times capital punishment was explicitly seen as a way of promoting social order. The new, relatively more "humane" guillotine was extolled because "the grandeur and elegance of the spectacle will attract many more people to the place of execution; more people will be unpressed, and the rule of law will be more greatly respected." In contemporary times, as the social order breaks down in countries such as Nigeria, public executions have become very popular: when increasing poverty tempts millions to theft, the execution of thieves validates the law abiding citizen's choice to stay "poor but honest."

Physical punishment, then, is not inhuman. It is a manifestly human way of forcing deviant or recalcitrant individuals to reintegrate into society, to become, again, confirming social being rather than threatening individuals. Torture is used on actual deviants and execution is displayed to potential deviants for lack of "better," less physical and more psychological means of enforcing confirmity. Personal sadism is not at the root of torture. Even the Nazi Gestapo, undoubtedly one of the cruelest organizations of torturers ever to exist, was interested in Soviet methods of punishment. Presumably this was because the Soviet secret police had devised sophisticated psychological means of extracting confession, conformity, and acknowledgment of the legitimacy of the Stalinist moral order that did not rely on physical torture. While some sadistic Nazis enjoyed torture for its own sake, for others torture was merely a means in an extreme situation to create the new Aryan community to which individualism, privacy, and autonomy were a threat.

The moral order, then, is a substantial part of the culture that is so frequently extolled by relativists as that which makes societies "unique." Societies are not unique, however, while the particularities of their customs, norms, and beliefs can be fascinating, they are forbidden by sociological regularities. The existence of culture itself is one such social regularity.

In the societies, there is a culture foundation. It consists of the customs, norms, values, and beliefs inculcated by one generation into the next. An important social function of culture is to teach the young the rules of status in society. Differentiating along status lines, the youngster learns how much deference to pay to different categories of adult and the appropriate demeanor with which to conduct himself or herself various situations. The young white South African, for example, learns that the deference he shows as a child to his black nanny must be replaced by an arrogant, superior demeanor by the time he reaches adolescence. Culture frequently underpins notions of human dignity radically at odds with the concept of human rights. Most cultures distinguish the degrees of respect owed to different status groups and certainly do not teach their young that all human beings, regardless of social origin or category, deserve equal treatment. The obvious North American example is the segregation practices of the U.S. South, not overturned in law until the 1960s and still constituting powerful social norms, sanctions, and taboos. Such legal segregation also existed in Canada until at least 1965.

A cultural relativist position, then, can easily become a philosophical stance that denies the universality of human rights. All societies do have underlying conceptions of human dignity and social justice. These conceptions can be identified; and certain commonalities of belief, for example, in the social value of work, can also be located on a transcultural basis. But in most known human societies, dignity and justice are not based on any idea of the *inalienable right* of the *physical*, socially *equal* human being against the claims of family, community, or the state. They are based on just the opposite, that is, the *alienable privileges* of *socially unequal* beings, considered to embody gradation of humanness according to socially, defined status categories entitled to different degrees of respect.

While all societies have underlying concepts of dignity and justice, few have concepts of rights. Human rights, then, are a particular expression of human dignity. In most societies, dignity does not imply human rights. There is very little cultural let alone universal foundation for the concept, as opposed to the content, of human rights. The society that actively protects rights both in law and in practice is a radical departure for most known human societies. Most rights-protective societies are explicitly a product of the liberal tradition that involved after the eighteenth century in Europe, and they are the products of social change that, both structurally and ideologically, was so disruptive as to create an almost entirely new conception of the human being.

Social Change and Human Rights

To discuss all of the various changes that took place, first in Western Europe and the settler colonies, then beyond, to bring about the new social order characterized in principle, if not yet in practice, by human rights, is beyond the scope of this chapter. Briefly, however, the changes in the conception of the human being can be summarized as follows. The key change is the development of a concept of the human being as *private* and individual.

Structural changes in the economy, briefly characterized as capitalism, induced concomitant changes in the way people lived. The change is summarized most succinctly in the sociological dichotomization of all societies into two "ideal types" "traditional" and "modern." Although this dichotomy is extremely crude and does injustice: in the vast array of non capitalist, non-Western societies that exist, it does nonetheless capture an existential shift in the way human beings (first men, then later and more rarely, women) thought of themselves.

Modernization entails changes in relations of human beings to the natural world. Property, held by communities that used it in accordance with their need is transformed into an individual possession that can be entirely disconnected from need and from the community's claims upon it. The connection of the community with nature is broken; the communal order no longer represents the natural order. Land and things become commodities to be bought and sold. People also become commoditized; social obligations among unequal give way to a market in labour power in which the purchaser has no obligations to the seller other than to pay an agreed-upon wage.

As the relation of the human to the natural world changes, so also does the relation of the human to the spiritual world. The development of science and technology allows men to control nature directly, without the continued mediation of the gods. A rupture between the individual human soul and the collective spirit occurs, the man in control of a machine no longer relies clearly on his priest. Both private property and private accumulaticm of knowledge (as a substitute for religiously based magic) contribute to the emergence of the modern private individual. If he does not become an outright atheist car agnostic, the private man is frequently attracted by more individualistic type of religion. Protestants communicate directly and silently with God in prayer; the priest no longer mediates for forgiveness of their sins.

The home becomes, for such a private man, his inner sanctum, his castle, over which he rules as the medieval lord ruled his manor. Private property permits the acquisition of wealth, with the consequent accumulation of personal goods. But since it also) allows for inheritance by one's own offspring, rather than redistribution to the community, such wealth is often invested in the private domain, inaccessible to the wider society but tangible to and inheritable by one's descendants. The obligation to the group, and to the group's gods, fades: the obligation to self and one's immediate family is strengthened.

Nor is the Individual as reliant on the group for knowledge as his forefathers. As literacy spreads, knowledge can be, and is, acquired privately. Methods of socialization are increasingly privatized and increasingly vary by social class or in position in the economy. Elite children are educated in their homes or in private academies. Even "public" education systems reflect class and other distinctions that remove individuals from cohesive social groups.

The ideal capitalist, then, is an individualized, private, autonomous creature. He seeks to make his own decisions on the basis of his own judgment: he objects to government "restrictions" on his autonomy even as he expects the government to safeguard his private interests. As his becomes the polincally and economically dominant class, his values spread to the entire society. Status-based distractions give way to a new stress on achievement that allows capitalists, regardless of their social origin, to demand respect for individual accomplishments. Earned money becomes more prestigious than inherited money, and the social order of inherited status disappears. These changes take place all over the world as the capitalist, private-oriented competitive economy spreads. In Ghana, for example, private entrepreneurs increasingly chafe at the restrictions upon the use of their wealth implied by their membership in wider communities of village or ethnic group.

The idea of privacy, then, is not universal; it is little known in precapitalist societies. Without privacy, one cannot develop a sense of the human individual as an intrinsically valuable being, abstracted from his or her social role. Indeed, this is evident in the manner by which different social groups have claimed rights even in the modern era. Women, insofar as they have been considered the embodiments of home and hearth, first had to extricate themselves from this connection and claim their right to privacy and autonomy before they could claim human rights.

Societies that accept the legitimacy of rights claims are modern and atypical. Most known human societies deny privacy, deny autonomy, and especially deny individualism. Socially induced conformity, public living, and collective, stratified decision-making are far more typical of human social existence than the rights-based societies that human rights activists wish were now the universal norm. Such a norm would, in practice, protect individuals in the modern world against the state and against other abusers of rights (such as the patriarch with his control of women and children). But although universally applicable in principle, the human rights norm is not universally locatable in practice or ideology.

The Challenge of Human Rights

The concept of human rights challenges both the ideal of community and, in those societies that are not liberal or individualist in orientation, the ideal of dignity. Dignity frequently means acceptance of social rules and norms; human rights implies challenge to precisely those norms. Dignity is often associated with social constraint, whereas human rights are associated with autonomy and freedom. As Orlando Patterson put it in his analysis of the connection between slavery (dishonour and natal alienation) and freedom, only slaves those completely removed from society were able to conceive, originally, of the value of such removal and its possibilities for autonomous freedom (individual rights):

> *Before slavery people simply could not have conceived of the thing we call freedom. Men and women in premodern, nonslaveholding societies did not, could not, value the removal of restraint as an ideal. Individuals yearned only for the security of being positively anchored in a network of power and authority. Happiness was membership: being was belonging.*

In earlier work I have argued that a liberal or perhaps better, a social democratic human rights regime is characterized by the autonomy, equality, and respect accorded to the individual. Human rights challenge the basis on which people in non-liberal societies accord each other *respect*. In such societies, respect was and is frequently a strictly graded matter of degree. One's ascriptively defined natal status influences the degree of respect to which one is entitled; so does one's conformity to one's proper social role. Finally, one's achievements for example in battle, as a political leader, or as an accumulator and distributor of wealth can also influence the degree of respect to which one is entitled. But respect merely because one is human, and for no other reason, is usually absent. Witness, for example, the treatment of children as "nonpersons" or merely persons information in most societies, and the very recent evolution of the idea that children too ought to have specifically defined rights.

The bases on which respect is accorded in non-liberal societies frequently violate the principle of *equality*. In liberal or social democratic political regimes, all citizens must in principle be accorded equal respect; in practice, of course, this principle is frequently violated. Nevertheless, the principle in and of itself challenges not only the organizing principles of past preliterate or precapitalist societies, but also the organizing principles of other types of communally-based societies, such as those communist societies that allocate benefits on the basis of real or perceived class origin.

Finally, the liberal principle of *autonomy* challenges the organizing bases of politics in all societies that hold principles of hierarchical authority, whether directed by elders or chiefs in primitive societies, or by party or dictator in modern ones. The principle of autonomy also challenges community-based principles of authority, the example, deference to priests or elders; and finally, it challenges patriarchal control in the family itself, as younger males, wives, and children claim rights against the father.

Conservatism and Dignity

Nevertheless, the notion of human dignity enshrined in ideological principle in liberal and social democratic societies is rarely practiced in full, if at all. Canada is a case in point, as a liberal society with social-democratic leanings. The overriding social division in Canada is stratification by wealth and income levels. The respect accorded among Canadians to each other is in practice largely a function of wealth, and the poor suffer from extreme everyday assaults on their dignity. The formal political equality of universal suffrage cannot compensate either for economic inequality or for formal inequalities of access to the political process. Finally, autonomy implies not only the capacity for individual thought, but also a chance that thought can he realized in action; and such autonomy, for many of Canada's poor, is completely absent.

Nor is Canada, even as a liberal society, completely innocent even of one of the most extreme denials of human equality and rights, namely racism. Rights-based regimes are everywhere extremely fragile, and ethnocentric exclusions of strangers from the rights bargain are common even in societies where universal citizenship is supposed to preclude ethnic or "racial" (phenotypical) discrimination. As is well known, Canada did not open its doors to refugee Jews strangers to the dominant Christian society during World War II. The treatment of both non-citizen and citizen ethnic Japanese in Canada during World War II replicated the early stage of what Helen Fein identified as the process of European genocide. Japanese were defined, stripped of property, segregated, and partially isolated; according to Fein, the only other intervening steps before extermination of European Jews were complete isolation and concentration.

Finally, Canada's past and current treatment of First Nation or "Native" peoples could be interpreted as cultural, if not physical, genocide. The Genocide Convention of 1948 defines genocide as any of the following acts committed *with intent to destroy*, in whole or in part, a national, ethnical, racial or religious group, as such:

A. killing members of the group;
B. causing serious bodily or mental harm;
C. deliberately inflicting on the group conditions of life calculated to bring about its physical destruction;
D. imposing, measures intended to prevent births;
E. forcibly transferring children of the group to another group.

While the issue of intent could be debated in the Canadian context, all of the above measures except possibly (d) (assuming that the high rates of sterilization of Native women have not been actual policy measures) have been inflicted upon Canada's Native peoples at various times since contact with European settlers, including the present.

That the liberal principles of human rights continue to be violated in practice in Canada and other liberal societies is not surprising. The conservative values of community and family still motivate many Canadians, as for example, the establishment of the "REAL" (family-oriented) Women of Canada movement, and the Christian Heritage Party in the Hamilton, Ontario, area in the last few years testifies. The stress on community and patriarchal family is easily compatible with ethnocentrism. In most societies, there are strong divisions between insiders and outsiders. In preliterate societies people not belonging to established ancestrally based or patron-client networks are generally considered to be strangers, and sometimes they are considered natural slaves.

In liberal societies, the only distinction that is supposed to be made is between citizen and alien; hence the continued questions in Canada, for example, of whether alien refugee claimants should be accorded the full legal protections automatically available in principle to any Canadian citizen. Citizenship is a legal category not intuitively, recognizable by many Canadians who continue to think in terms of cultural group membership, and to acknowledge as their equals in practice only those who are co members of their same "racial" (phenotypical), ethnic, linguistic and/or religious group. In 1981, for example, some 31 percent of Canadians said they would support a whites-only Canada. Under such circumstances "self-determination in the sphere of membership" (i.e., the right of a community to decide who shall join it) can easily violate basic human rights provisions for non-discrimination. The demand for collective rights can become a mask for conservative attempts to retain discriminatory communities that deny equal and individual human rights.

Potential Incompatibility of Human and Collective Rights

In the following discussion I distinguish between the move for aboriginal rights, which I support as necessary for the preservation of non capitalist land tenure and productive relations essential to retention of the identity of "Native" groups already subject to several centuries of physical and cultural genocide, and the move for collective or peoples' rights. My remarks concern the latter category insofar as it does not apply to the rights of conquered peoples in settled capitalist societies. My remarks are meant to express doubts, not an absolute rejection of the concept of collective rights.

It is dangerous to assume that collective rights are compatible with, or perhaps even superior to, individual human rights. Collective rights can become exclusivist rights. They establish communities and define on bases other than universalist citizenship who is or is not a member of them. The result can be what Michael McDonald calls "tragic choices." For example, the inclusion of peoples' rights in the African Charter of Rights runs the risk of legitimating Sierra Leone's practice of denying citizenship to native-born ethnic non-Africans (usually of Lebanese origin). Many Arab citizens of the state of Israel consider that its ethnoreligious basis results in inequalities and indignities; for example, they consider Israel's holidays "irrelevant at best, irritating and insulting at worst," and also hold the view that the Law of Return (allowing Jews from anywhere in the world to become Israeli citizens) discriminates against Arabs born in Palestine, who, in their view, have a stronger ancestral claim to Israeli citizenship than most Jews born outside the Middle East. The assertion of collective, community, or people's right does not simply mean an extra right of individuals to belong to intact communities that embody their own cultural identity. Such assertion also can, and frequently does, mean violation of individual rights.

Not only does the notion of people's rights or collective rights suggest automatic denial of rights to individuals who could be considered noncitizens by virtue of place of origin, it also implies the risk of progressive exclusion of categories of individuals internal to a national society from membership in the community. It must not be forgotten that the most extreme Western example of social exclusion, Nazism, underwent precisely this type of progressive definition of nonmembers of the community. The Nazis adopted pseudoscientific Social Darwinist theories that permitted them to murder "defective" Aryan (German Christian) children and adults even before they began the mass murder of Jews, the Romany people (gypsies), any blacks they could find in conquered Europe, Slavic prisoners of war, homosexuals, and other categories of persons. But Nazism was also, deeply rooted in the idea of ascriptively based membership in the localized community as opposed to individualistic egalitarian citizenship. This opposition, in Nazi thought, was exemplified in the dichotomous categorization of *Volk* (people) versus *cosmopolitan*. The cosmopolitan Jew exemplified the stranger at home in and (in Nazi ideology) controlling world civilization but not having any rootedness in the idealized *volkisch* peasant community from which the Aryan race was said to have sprung. Social Darwinism and volkisch ideology combined to produce an ever-tightening, exclusivist definition of the collectivity.

Communal or group rights then, are deeply attractive to those aspects even of the modern psyche that are nostalgic for the idealized closed, ordered community of our mythic rural past, that rigidity for which Mary Douglas believes we all yearn. Liberal capitalist societies do contain deeply disintegrative social aspects. Alienation of individuals from established social norms is frequent, and a sense of isolation plagues many modern men and women who no longer belong to established, easily identifiable social groups other than the nation itself. To such alienated people, the cultural (symbolic, normative) integrity of the group is frequently more appealing than the personal (intellectual, spiritual) integrity that they might be able to achieve as individuals.

The late twentieth-century ideology of individualism, embodied in beliefs that people can control their own fate, puts a tremendous strain on many people. One is now expected in the popular ideology to take "responsibility" for almost all aspects of one's own life, as if history, politics, economics, and social structure have no meaning. One takes "responsibility" for one's own health through jogging, abstention from physical indulgences, and other such aspects of the fitness movement. One is supposed, moreover, to take charge of one's progress in the competitive economic marketplace through manipulation of the symbolic aspects of success (dress, demeanor) as, well as through long hours of hard work. Finally, one's spiritual health is now also one's own responsibility: "self-fulfilment" is an individualized matter, depending on one's recognition and satisfaction of one's own "potential," abstracted from family or community.

Such a culturally, individualized society results in extreme strain for many people, a strain that can be overcome by a return to "fundamental" values of home, community, or church. Conservatism has its attractions even in a liberal or social democratic society. Human Rights can be compatible with a political conservatism that accepts the fundamental principles of rights even while, in the political marketplace, asking for more attention to be paid to family and community. When conservatism denies the fundamentally individual aspect of human rights, however, then it is positing a radically different notion of human dignity and social justice.

It is in this sense that human (individual) rights and collective rights are incompatible. Human rights is, to repeat, one particular conception of human dignity and social justice. It is not synonymous, despite their joining in the Universal, Declaration of Human Rights, with human dignity. All societies and all social and political philosophies have conceptions of human dignity. Some of these especially those rooted in the view that nation, "people," community, or family must take precedence over the individual are radically at odds with the idea of human rights. The recent tendency to substitute collective rights for human rights in international debate, or to assume that the two types of rights can exist compatibly, fails to note this crucial difference.

Summary

To look for an anthropologically based consensus on the content of human rights is to miss the point. There may be aspects of agreement worth noting among what many societies take to be fundamental to a life of dignity and what the modern notion of human rights includes as its content. The concept of human rights is not universal in origin, however; and it cannot be located in most societies. The human being free and equal to all others regardless of status or achievement, and permitted to make individualist claims against state, community, and family is unthinkable in many societies, however, much he or she may be in dire need of rights in the modern world.

6

Human Rights Abuses in Fledgling Democracies

Introduction

A new campaign of police abuse has met with little public reaction, and in the 1991 elections, candidates representing extremely authoritarian views had an astonishing appeal. Military officers running for provincial governorships and seats in the lower house captured a substantial portion of the electorate. This appeal was not diminished by the fact that these candidates had either represented the delinquent military dictatorship in the same jurisdictions where they were running in 1991 or had stood up against the elected government of President Raul Alfonsín to have the trials terminated.

The most surprising event was the success of ex-Lieutenant-Colonel Aldo Rico, who ran for governor of the Buenos Aires province in the September 10, 1991 elections. Rico had been cashiered during the Alfonsin administration for leading military rebellions against his commanders in April 1987 and January 1988. Pardoned by President Saul

Menem in 1989, hardly anybody considered him or his newly founded party, MODIM, as having a chance of obtaining over 2 percent of the electorate in Buenos Aires. Identified with a staunchly undemocratic faction of the Army, Rico's party obtained three seats at the National Congress when almost 11 percent of the province's population voted for his ticket. This is particularly astonishing considering that Rico headed revolts in an attempt to remove the Army's commanders for failing to stop the trials of officers accused of violating human rights. According to Rico, such failure jeopardized the dignity of the Army. After the elections, most political observers conjectured that the success of Rico's party was a desperate move by the urban poor of Buenos Aires province. Recent polls have demonstrated, however, that the ex-officer's voters were mostly middle class.

Another striking example involves General Domingo Bussi. In the northern province of Tucumán, where he earned a grim reputation for the assassination of prisoners as the delegate of the 1976-83 dictatorship, Bussi obtained 43 percent of the vote, but still lost to the Peronist Party candidate, pop singer Ramon ("Palito") Ortega, whom Menem backed personally. Bussi challenged the elections, claiming they had been rigged. This opinion is shared by many observers who suspect the rigging occurred because of the federal government appointee who supervised the elections in Tucuman.

My own conclusion is that if genuine (institutional) authority is not asserted in Argentina, democracy cannot be expected to be more than formal, and strong leaders will maintain their appeal to large sectors of this fragmented society. The lack of initial clarity concerning the purposes and limits of the human rights trials, rapidly followed by immunity, and the pardon decrees of 1989 and 1990 in particular, undermined the reliability of Congress and the judiciary. To understand the ultimate outcome of the policies of the transitional governments, a short review of the

Alfonsín government's policy regarding the human rights violations of the prior military juntas is required.

Justifications for the Trials

Raúl Alfonsín was elected president of Argentina in 1983, replacing a series of military juntas that were responsible for grave human rights abuses during the 1970s, including assassinations, arbitrary detention, and the forced disappearance of at least 10,000 people. Alfonsín quickly instituted a series of measures aimed at investigating and prosecuting human rights violators and providing redress for victims. He created the National Commission on Disappeared Persons (CONADEP), headed by novelist Ernesto Sabato, and charged it with investigating the fate of those who had disappeared. Although it was unable to subpoena witnesses or compel testimony, the Commission produced a detailed and widely read report, *Nunca Más.*

Another central plank of the Alfonsín government's platform was the trial of persons considered responsible for the campaign of disappearances and assassinations. Trying the military required annulling, as void, *ab initio,* a self-serving amnesty law that had been issued by executive decree shortly before the military left power. Once the judiciary annulled the amnesty law, cases of human rights violations by the military were to be tried initially before the Supreme Council of the Armed Forces, with appeal to the civilian courts. The Law to Amend the Code of Military Justice, enacted on February 9, 1984, gave the military court 180 days to complete each trial, made appeal to civilian courts mandatory, and exculpated those who had acted under orders, unless they had exceeded those orders or had committed "atrocious and aberrant acts." This initial due obedience clause did not prevent prosecutions, because whether defendants had committed the prohibited acts could be established only by trial on the merits. The idea was to allow the military to cleanse itself. This approach proved to be a mistake, however, as the military courts dithered after indicting some of the members of the first two juntas but refused later to pursue the cases further. Eventually the cases of human rights violations were removed to civilian courts, but valuable time, and a reservoir of political support, had been lost.

In deciding whom to prosecute, the government focused on the commanders of the three branches of the armed services, who had made up the members of the governing juntas. In December 1984, the federal court of appeals of Buenos Aires took over the conduct of the trials against the commanders. After a highly publicized five-month trial, the court sentenced General Jorge Videla and Admiral Emilio Massera to life imprisonment and three other junta members to terms of sixteen, eight, and four years and acquitted four others. The Supreme Court upheld the decision in December 1986. Several other high-ranking military officers were also tried.

As time went on, however, the bulk of the military became increasingly opposed to the trials, and protests from the military sectors were accompanied by bomb blasts throughout the country. Under pressure, the government had pushed through Congress a law known as the *punto final*, or "full stop" which limited new complaints brought for crimes committed during the dirty war to a sixty-day period; existing complaints would be considered moot unless the courts took action during that time. The result was a flurry of complaint filings by human rights groups and victims' families. The law was insufficient to quell military unrest, however, and in April 1987 a group of young Army officers, led by Lieutenant-Colonel Aldo Rico, took over a military compound after an officer accused of torture sought refuge there rather than face the questions of a civilian court. Although the government, backed by widespread popular support, put down the rebellion, months later it passed a "due obedience" law that had the effect of an amnesty for many potential defendants. This second law was aimed at appeasing the intermediate ranks who claimed that they were unjustly bearing the weight of the "dirty war." They claimed that they were being put to trial for their direct involvement in human rights violations, whereas their superior officers who had issued the orders but had neither designed nor carried them out remained untouched or were even promoted. This new initiative ensured that officers beneath the rank of colonel and some above that rank who did not hold positions as chiefs of security areas or forces would not be criminally prosecuted. It created an irrebuttable presumption that lower officers were following orders and thus were not liable. The Supreme Court promptly upheld the constitutionality of the law. Those officers excluded from the operation of the "due obedience" law, together with the convicted commanders, were pardoned by incoming President Saul Menem in decrees dated October 6, 1989 and December 29, 1990. Given the vagaries of the political context in which the commanders were tried and sentenced, the question as to the value of the trials is still a matter of speculation today.

There are several reasons for claiming that retributive sanctions will contribute to establishing democracy by reasserting the authority of institutions, largely the judiciary, thus awakening individuals' sense of their rights. Trying state criminals affirms the principle that nobody is beyond the reach of the law and that citizens have rights the exercise of which is essential to a working democracy. By this token transitional administrations have a moral obligation to try persons responsible for human rights violations. As one who has argued this way, I have claimed that punishment plays an important role in reversing the citizens' adaptation to a dictatorial system in which fear drove them from pursuing their ideals and political activities, into apathy, isolation, and self-disdain. A rights-based community is unlikely to emerge from populations in which persecution and fear compelled individuals to give up their personal values and ideals. To limit the category of victims of repression to those who disappeared, the tortured, and the jailed ignores the social repercussions of state crime. Protracted repression not only caused pain and anguish to those who were related to or associated with the murdered and the disappeared but it also debased the large majority of the population. Brutality brings about a culture of fear and insecurity that pervades the community at large. The notion that almost everybody qualifies for state abuses penetrated most aspects of social life.

Fear demands adjustment. Afraid that by the most whimsical criteria they will become victims of repression, individuals break social ties and throw away any possibly "incriminating evidence," such as books, that could link them to the left. In dictatorial regimes, the state systematically represses the pursuit of individual ideals and values it considers undesirable. As members of the community abandon walks of life that make existence meaningful to them, they surrender self-respect and self-esteem. This feature of dictatorships represents one of the most burdensome legacies transitional governments must overcome and often leads to an inescapable paradox. The crueler the infringements, the more retributive justice is needed; yet the more retributive justice is needed, the less the courts will retain whatever authority they might have had. Prospects for impartial justice depend on a community's sense of moral responsibility, and this sense is determined by individuals' perception of their own worth and by authoritative institutions that ensure and promote that perception. Minimally, state repression blurs such perception.

As an argument against prosecuting military officers, a sizable number of Argentine politicians claimed from 1983 on that allotting resources to avert future violations was the state's priority. But the choice of not trying human rights violators and securing respect for individual rights in the future is nonexistent. The failure to exact punishment on state criminals will, in and of itself, frustrate attempts to lessen society's authoritarian tendencies. Citizens who bore or feared to bear persecution are not likely to spontaneously develop self respect once the dictatorship is over. Incapable of self-respect, they will also deem other people's choices unworthy.

The oppressor kills our ideals, our self-respect, the perception of our rights. Compromising our goals makes us feel shame; deserting our principles and loyalties instills guilt in us. Our sense of worthlessness, of shame, and of guilt demands a "political remedy." Only public admission by political institutions that we were wronged will legitimize us in our own eyes. Punishment of the violators of our rights is the clearest and strongest statement an authoritative institution may issue to that effect. Citizens need to learn that they have rights not only to be able to act on these rights but to respect other people's liberties as well. A rights based community is unlikely to emerge spontaneously from populations in which individuals adapted to dictatorial violence by giving up their personal values and ideals. Two reasons to punish those responsible for these practices seem self-evident. First, trials of human rights abusers will expectedly generate awareness of recent history, and this recognition is a prerequisite for effecting change. Second, brutal repression not only causes anguish for those directly touched by the assassinations but it also deeply affects the large majority of the population. Public admission that a large sector of society was wronged will help legitimize government institutions in the eyes of the citizens; and punishment of human rights violators is the most authoritative and strongest statement to that effect.

But the policy of trying "state criminals" has visible weaknesses. First, experience has revealed the difficulties posed by selecting those persons to be brought to trial. An inevitable air of artificiality surrounds establishing the boundaries of responsibility. By pinning the blame on a limited sector of society, human rights trials reinvent history. The meaning of the resulting "truth" inevitably becomes controversial if not plainly factious. Dissatisfaction with the Argentine trials was conveyed not only by those who defended the convicted officers but also by human rights activists such as the Madres de Plaza de Mayo. While the former claimed the culprits were scapegoats, the latter protested that too few of the accused were actually convicted and that their sentences were too light. For both parties, the trials were clearly political: Instead of bringing about justice, the judiciary was adjusting to the political convenience of the executive.

The most perplexing feature of this fragmentation of public opinion as a result of the lack of authoritativeness of the courts is that few people, including lawyers, ground their positions on the December 1985 decision of the federal appellate court of Buenos Aires concerning the responsibility of the military juntas that ruled the country between 1976 and 1982. The verdict of the Supreme Court, delivered one year later, is equally irrelevant to the citizenry's view of its recent political history. This verdict shows that despite the theoretical claim that a judicial determination will establish an authoritative truth, in Argentina judicial decisions lack authoritativeness both in establishing the facts brought to trial and in evaluating these facts. Thus, controversies about what should have been done about past human rights violations continue unabated, with no hope that any arbiter will bring them to an end.

The Argentine judiciary lacks authority for many reasons. One reason is a general distrust of the impartiality of the courts in trying politically related cases that arise during dictatorial periods. I believe there are three reasons specifically connected to the human rights trials: (1) the absence of a clear idea of how the human rights trials may have contributed to the democratization of the Argentine polity; (2) the inevitable shortcomings of truncated and selective prosecutions; and (3) the lack of an adequate system of prosecutorial discretion.

Victim-Centered Theory of Punishment

I have argued elsewhere that neither a deterrence-based nor a full-blooded retributivist rationale for punishment adequately applies in cases of state crimes. I do not claim that the examined utilitarian and retributivist approaches do not contribute to the justification for punishing state criminals. Utilitarians are correct to expect criminal convictions to have dissuasive effects. But at their best these effects are, as I have explained, limited to a few officers at the top. Retributivists also provide a cogent argument for protecting individual rights: Persons who are not guilty of wrongful acts ought not be punished. This negative aspect of retributivism is modest; it refers solely to restraints on the utilization of punishment. It does not offer a (positive) justification for criminal convictions. I have argued that punishment should contribute to the making of a rights-based democracy. I have also suggested that institutional regard for the victims of crime is crucial to the furtherance of that goal. In that respect, utilitarianism and full-blooded retributivism, as "perpetrator-centered" theories, are intrinsically inappropriate. I propose a "victim-centered" theory of punishment as an independent ground for justifying the conviction of state criminals.

Redress for victims is nonessential to a utilitarian justification. By giving key significance to the deterrence of potential offenders, utilitarians will have no qualms about overlooking the plight of persons who have suffered degradation as a consequence of having their basic rights infringed upon or threatened. The notion of justice for the victims would be excluded from the utilitarian calculus when discretion is exercised. Full-blooded retributivists invite a similar criticism. By disregarding all consequences of punishment, proponents of this version of retributivism focus only on wrongdoers' facing the consequences of their deeds.

But there is another variant of retributivism a goal-oriented variant. According to this version, punishment ought to be directed at redressing the valued sentiments of those who were wronged. I am not referring to vindictive sentiments but rather to the victims' loss of a sense of purpose and of their own worth. As I have explained, the persons who endured unwarranted actual or potential chastisement from the oppressor experience feelings of shame and a lack of self-respect for renouncing the personal ideals that made their lives meaningful. Goal-oriented retributivists will attach to punishment the function of restoring this lost trust.

There is a salient pragmatic difference between full-blooded and goal-oriented retributivists. Whereas the former are compelled to impose punishment given the presence of a set of conditions that render an act criminal, such generality does not apply to goal-oriented retributivists. In seeking redress for the victims, the latter may consistently choose to forgo punishment or else content themselves with merely condemning the offender or solely the offender's deed. If goal-oriented retributivists believe that imposing pain upon the perpetrator will do nothing substantial to improve the victim's sense of self-respect and confidence, punishment will lack warrant. So if the victims of certain forms of state crimes have already regained self-respect and are confident that they will be protected against future violations because the heads of the criminal organization have been convicted, goal-oriented retributivists may refrain from punishing other members of the group. There is room for considerable discretion. This discretion would legitimately allow a transitional government, for example, to limit prosecutions to certain heinous offenses, to the most notorious perpetrators, or to those individuals most closely associated with the design and implementation of a policy of terror.

Thus, moral justification exists for the "full stop" law proposed by President Alfonsin.

Nonetheless, I believe that the 1985 trials did not adequately employ the approach to punishment espoused here. On the one hand, some officers, such as the members of the last junta, were known to have had no direct responsibility over the scattered abuses perpetrated shortly before the government was handed over to elected authorities. On the other hand, generals whom overwhelming evidence singled out as the protagonists of the worst acts of repression were also tried for forgery and usurpation of property. These offenses have no connection with gross human rights abuses and are not comparable in either nature or moral gravity, thus blurring the lessons of the trials. At the same time, the mid- and upper-level officers who were most deeply involved in planning and executing the crimes at a regional and local level were exempted. Although admittedly prosecuting all 2,000 or so officers and their civilian aides and instigators involved in one way or another was impossible, if the Alfonsin government had, for example, initially prosecuted a larger group of some sixty to one hundred officers, the lesson would have been clearer. As it was, the initial choice of a few officers, and the subsequent restrictions and later forgoing of their punishment, had the opposite effect on many victims. The trials also blurred the citizenry's perception of recent history.

Blaming as Social Practice

Both official and popular versions of recent Argentine history suggest that state sponsored human rights violations were the result of the military regime's strategy following its 1976 takeover. However, situating the massive abuses between March 1976 and December 1983, when the military was formally in power, is a misguiding version of that history. State violence actually began in the early 1970s. Felt to be a necessary response to the activities of insurgent groups that had emerged in the late 1960s, a large portion of the middle class supported a wave of assassinations and abductions perpetrated by paramilitary gangs directly associated with the elected Peronist government in office. Peron's minister of social welfare, José Lopez Rega, ran the most prominent of these groups, the Triple A, aided by factions in the police, the Army, and right-wing civilians. Between 1974 and the end of 1975 hardly a day passed without reports of disappearances and assassinations.

Immediately after the military takeover of March 1976, assassinations by the Army and the security forces increased, and a wave of abductions many performed in broad daylight rocked the country. Labelled as subversives, the targets of state-sponsored terrorism were varied: workers, students, writers, lawyers, and even priests and nuns.

The military was not alone in staging the "antisubversive" campaign. A rightwing sector of the citizenry actively contributed to brutal repression as paramilitary squads and vigilante groups. Conspicuous members of the Catholic Church praised the assassination of students and workers by underscoring the spiritual value of the crusade and the "patriotic merit of eliminating the 'unrecuperable elements' of society." Beyond these organized groups, the middle class actively or passively supported state brutality. A vast sector of the population justified the official strategy by either denying what was happening or pinning the blame for torture and assassinations on the victims themselves. Whenever someone disappeared one was often confronted with the phrase, "There is something she must have done" or, "She must have been up to something," placing the blame on the victim and not on the perpetrator. This social environment is vividly described in the Prologue to *Nunca Mas, the official report of the Commission on the Disappearance of People, headed by writer Ernesto Sábato:*

The idea of insecurity became increasingly entrenched in society: the dark fear that anybody, no matter how innocent, could fall victim to that infinite witch hunt. Some were absorbed by overwhelming fear, while others were controlled by the conscious or unconscious proclivity to justify horror: "There is something she must have done" was the whisper, as wanting to favour inscrutable gods, looking at the children or parents of the disappeared as if they were pest ridden. These sentiments were vacillating, because it was known that so many had been swallowed up by that abyss without bottom without being guilty of anything; because the struggle against the "subversive," with the drift that characterizes the hunting of witches and the possessed, had turned into a dementia! generalized repression. Because the epithet "subversive" had such a vast and unpredictable reach.

The initiation of state-sponsored terrorism by right-wing activists most of them civilians before the 1976 military takeover, active participation of civilians in the campaign of terror during the military dictatorship, and mass support of the citizenry of the dictatorship's campaign of terror demonstrate that responsibility was shared by many sectors of society. The persistent appeal of violence indicates that the 1983 collective demand that the "military assassins" (milicos asesinos) be punished was based on a (conscious or unconscious) biased representation of past events. The moral and legal responsibility for Argentina's tragic past appears to be oversimplified by narrowly ascribing political terror to the military and by limiting it to the abuses perpetrated by military officers during the 1976-83 dictatorship. This rationalized reinterpretation explains why one of the judges responsible for convicting military officers for human rights abuses confessed to me in private: "I often feel we have treated the military like scapegoats. It is now clear to me we have done nothing about the civilians who marched with the military and later turned their backs upon them."

In many cases "fault" is not the result of our causal findings but rather an identifiable, "external," "aberrant" element that makes social events intelligible. In this latter sense, in the seventies a large sector of Argentine society "understood" massive disappearances and torture by placing blame on the victims and their conjectured behaviour: "She must have been up to something." In the eighties this "understanding" changed radically as blame for these abuses shifted to the military as a group clearly disconnected from the rest of society: "milicos asesinos." Yet narrowly connected to our political interests, the social practice of blaming is a selective process by which we attempt to control the behaviour of the people we blame. Intimately related to the balance of power, blaming is essentially the practice one sector of society uses to change some other sector's future conduct. Earlier in Argentina it was left-wing students, progressive trade union leaders, and workers. Later it was the military.

In part, narrowing the focus of blame was the result of partisan political interests rather than the more "sincere" outcome of an open debate that would reflect the far more complex and wider allocation of responsibility. The issue of blame was tied to a host of political restrictions in 1983, the most important being avoiding direct confrontation with the largest opposition group the Peronist Party, which ruled between 1973 and 1976. The fledgling democracy had too much to lose by clashing with the Peronists, who were temporarily allied in order to press for general elections. Thus, blaming deepened political conflict and further fragmented the social perception of reality.

In part, too, the very mechanism of trials divides the world into *guilty* and *innocent*, with those not declared guilty judged to be innocent of the terror campaign regardless of their direct or indirect involvement in the campaign or in the creation of the political environment that led to it. On the one hand, this process led necessarily to the view that only a limited number of citizens were responsible for the extreme violence the country had experienced; on the other hand, the process led to a perceived scapegoating as members of a sector were accused by, among others, those who also should have shared the brunt of a widely supported strategy. It thus perpetuated the "us versus them" war mentality that makes one's political adversaries the proper subjects of repressive measures.

Role of the Judiciary

Like the criminal justice systems of most Latin American countries, Argentina's adopted the so-called principle of legality. According to this principle, neither the prosecutors nor the courts are entitled to dismiss cases that are legally defined as criminal. Cogent with the full-blooded retributivist tradition, actions defined as crimes create the duty to prosecute and convict. This feature of the country's law poses a serious obstacle to the credibility of judges when they are trying state sponsored human rights violations. In such situations, the perpetrators who must stand trial usually a large number of people and the corporatist powers behind them, impose overwhelming pressure upon the judiciary. In Argentina, while the military and their supporters pressed for acquittals, vast sectors of the population demanded convictions. Under such circumstances, putting the judiciary in the spotlight turned the judiciary itself into the centerpiece of one of Argentina's most critical political struggles. The military pompously called this struggle the judicial battle.

Judges during the transitional period in the establishment of a democracy play the key role of instilling among the citizenry a sense of self-respect and the respect of other people by making rights an essential part of the political arrangement. This idea, I think, is a sufficient reason to refrain from passing amnesty laws. Placing the judges at the center of the transitional process by having them bear the weight of such significant political conflict, however, threatens to jeopardize the impartiality of the judiciary, given the intensity of the debate that takes place outside the courtroom. During my tenure in office, a day did not pass when I did not receive numerous telephone calls or visits from people who had strong views on these issues. Indeed, these individuals often expressed concern if not alarm about the upheaval the human rights trials were causing within the armed forces, the negative impact that trying certain officers would have on their comrades, or the "senselessness" of confronting the most powerful sector of society.

Army officers and numerous politicians were apprehensive. Presidential military aides did not miss a single occasion to convey their alarm. High officials and an array of sympathizers with the military regime, and even personal friends among the civilians, shared concern about what the trials could lead to. Directly or indirectly, thousands of officers were implicated in human rights abuses. The reasons for urging restraint in the scope of the trials or for giving up the trials altogether ranged from practical grounds to ideological allegiances.

For the judges, the pressure placed on the judiciary by the trials of human rights violators rapidly became unbearable. As a consequence of the permanent pressure exerted by different sectors of society with direct interest in the outcome of the trials, the members of the Buenos Aires federal court gradually abandoned their life-tenured positions. By the end of 1987, that court had been replaced entirely by newly appointed judges. For many observers, the resignations of these judges severely undermined the credibility of the human rights trials. The military and their sympathizers viewed their move as an admission that the trials were politically biased and that once their mission of convicting a few generals was accomplished, some members of the tribunal would seek to aggrandize themselves by obtaining important government positions in the Alfonsín regime, whereas others successfully went into private practice. Although I do not believe there are serious grounds for defending such a thesis, the fact that one of the judges was appointed secretary of the interior and another attorney general by President Alfonsín himself makes it difficult to argue convincingly for the impartiality of the court.

Human rights organizations also believed that the court's decision had been tainted by an allegiance to the administration in power. They claimed that the sentences imposed upon some commanders were unjustifiably light and that the acquittal of other officers was a sign that the court had set out to help President Alfonsín in his undeclared effort to favour the armed forces by creating a facade of an impartial trial. History has confirmed, however, that it was impossible for the judges to have borne the burden of trying the sizable number of accused officers.

It is arguable that the pressure could have been ameliorated had the judges been conferred the power to select the cases to be tried. Such an approach, however, would not have been a solution because the pressure to impose sentences one way or another would have simply shifted to the point of deciding who would be tried; and suspicions would have been equally drawn from both quarters. The military would have still accused the court of turning those indicted into scapegoats. Human rights activists would have raised the objection that the exercise of discretion was but a masquerade of justice. The authoritativeness of the justice system depends to a great degree, then, on prosecutorial discretion.

Nor can an adequate selection of cases be made by individual prosecutors: The issue is too critical to be left to the temptations of quick political solutions adopted on the basis of expediency by the administration in power. Although practical reasons such as political necessity and limited resources make it crucial that the government have a say, it seems indispensable to merge short-term political views with farsighted policy making. Both Professor Julio Maier and Judge Andres D'Alessio suggested to me that a criminal policy department should be created in Argentina. The attorney general (or the solicitor general), as a member of the judiciary, and the ombudsman, or special prosecutor, would integrate this office together with that of the minister of justice. Whereas the latter would embody the government's immediate priorities, the former would represent society's long-term interests. Maier suggested that a board headed by the three officials could serve the purpose of exercising discretion.

The possibility of prosecutorial discretion, exercised in light of the victim-centered justifications I referred to earlier, would go some way toward imbuing judicial decisions with the authority they require if they are to serve a democratizing effect. Disregard for the victims as a reason to punish state criminals has been an important factor in the failure to transform an authoritarian society into a rights based community. But the dismal path the case for individual rights has taken in Argentina in the 1990s is also a consequence of not taking the judiciary seriously. Blatantly neutralizing convictions for human rights violations, Menem's pardons of officers undercut the nascent authority of the judiciary. Until such authority is restored, a rights-based society will never flourish in Argentina.

7

Human Rights in Romania

Introduction

The main source of pressure to settle accounts has come from a fragmented opposition, most fervently when a grass-roots movement emerged in the spring of 1990 with the expectation that it could influence the shape of the future regime through politics of protest. That chapter came to a close, however, when a newly elected government welcomed the assistance of miners from the Jiu Valley, who converged on Bucharest for the third and bloodiest time that year to restore order.

The emergence and consolidation of the new ruling clique proved to affect significantly Romania's ability to come to terms with the past. A true coming to terms would have required a difficult confrontation with a large, immovable bureaucracy and the *nomenklatura* from the prior regime. In Romania, that confrontation has been sharply tempered by Romanian leaders who themselves owe allegiance to the same bureaucracy and *nomenklatura*. Instead of fulfilling the expectations of many Romanians who were filled with revolutionary zeal and who expected a clean break with the past, the transitional regime manipulated public opinion with the false appearance of justice. The end result did nothing to end Romania's culture of impunity, inherited from the Ceausescu regime. The effects persist into the present.

The events of December 1989 are still clouded in mystery, and no one has been held accountable to the public for the bloody clashes that took place between miners and protestors in June 1990. The execution of the Ceausescus and the trials that followed the revolution may have satisfied an immediate thirst for revenge spawned by the violent turmoil or may have fulfilled the political needs of those in power. These actions did not, however, represent a coming to terms with the past or even the present.

Moreover, issues of decommunization or punishment of past human rights abuses are especially complex because Romania is in the midst of confronting a primary problem: establishing the truth about what happened (and what is happening). Indeed, "the truth" is a loaded term in Romania. Too often, generalized conclusions stand in for specific information. This attitude toward truth is deeply ingrained in the consciousness of the Romanian people: so much so that in late 1992, a group of young Romanian democrats proposed in all earnestness to tackle Romania's "image problem" by creating a centralized coordinating center for all independent non-governmental organizations, to be called "The Truth About Romania." The proposal demonstrated a failure to distinguish between discovering truth and creating it.

Ceausescu Falls and Justice Fails

The events surrounding the Romanian revolution of 1989 are so murky and controversial that many question even calling it a revolution. Many Romanians, when referring to the upheaval that accompanied the change in regime, speak of the "events of December" or *tulburarile* ("the disturbance.") The conspiracy theorists, who abound in Romania, postulate that December 1989 represented everything from a palace coup to a foreign intervention by security forces from Hungary, the Soviet Union, Israel, or the United States. Most observers agree, however, that what happened in Romania in December 1989 began as a genuine popular uprising, even if it was later seized by a political elite who could be most charitably described as an internal opposition within the ranks of the Communist Party, the Army, and the security apparatus.

The events of December began on December 16, 1989 in Timisoara, a town in southwest Romania close to the Hungarian and Serbian borders. On December 15, 1989 protests arose over the forced transfer from Timosoara of Bishop Laszlo Tokes of the Hungarian Reformed Church of Romania. Although the police were initially restrained, the protests soon escalated and troops opened fire on the demonstrators under orders that came directly from Nicolae Ceausescu and that were approved by the Political Executive Committee of the Communist Party (the Romanian equivalent of a Politburo). At least dozens of demonstrators were killed.

The Timisoara phone lines had been blocked, and the roads leading to Timisoara had been closed. Nevertheless, word was out by the time Ceausescu returned from a diplomatic visit to Iran on December 20. When he ill-advisedly called for a televised public demonstration the next day as a show of support, a small protest broke out in the back of the crowd. Caught off guard by the disruption, Ceausescu appeared to falter. The national television station interrupted its live coverage of the event for several minutes while order was restored, but not before some boos and catcalls could be heard and Ceausescu's vulnerability became obvious to the viewing public.

The people of Bucharest took the irregularities as their cue to go to the streets. Protest demonstrations formed at University Square and Romana Circle. Savage repression by the Army and security forces resulted in many deaths and injuries and continued into the early morning hours of

December 22, 1989. By daylight, however, the clashes had ended, and the Army together with some units of the Securitate appeared to have switched sides. People left their jobs en masse, and soon hundreds of thousands of people were in the streets, with the Army fraternizing with the crowds. Elena and Nicolae Ceausescu were forced to flee but were caught in Tirgoviste, a town northwest of Bucharest, later that day.

Videotapes later made public recorded the first meeting of the elite clique that constituted itself as the National Salvation Front that same afternoon. Ion Iliescu, elected five months later as Romania's first post-Communist president, had already emerged as the public face of the National Salvation Front, having signed the new entity's first public statement. He had been a prominent member of the *nomenklatura* and a high-ranking Communist Party official before being dismissed from the Central Committee in 1984. Others present at the first meeting included top-ranking generals and some of Ceausescu's closest advisers.

The arrest of the Ceausescus was announced by a spokesman for the newly formed National Salvation Front who promised a public trial. The next day, Iliescu confirmed the arrest in a televised speech. "The time will come for their just and harsh judgment by the people," he said.

New Regime Faces Its First Trial

The trial of the Ceausescus presented the new regime with its first opportunity to make a firm break with the abuses of the past and to provide a public accounting. That opportunity was lost. Instead, the Ceausescus were tried by a secret, specially constituted military tribunal, and the first official acknowledgement of their status came when the media broadcast a National Salvation Front statement three days after their arrest. Much later that night, Romanian television showed selected excerpts of the Ceausescus' trial and dramatic footage of the former ruling couple lying dead, with multiple bullet wounds, in pools of blood.

According to the videotape of the proceedings, most of the two-hour long trial consisted of bare accusations of crimes committed by the Ceausescus against the Romanian people and the Ceausescus' protests that they did not recognize the authority of the tribunal, that they had been victims of a foreign-sponsored coup, and that they should be heard by the Grand National Assembly. Ultimately they were accused of genocide, with over 60,000 victims, and of attempting to flee the country with foreign-held assets. They were formally convicted under articles 162, 163, 165, and 167 of the Romanian Penal Code for undermining state power through organization of armed actions, destroying public assets, undermining the national economy, and conspiracy.

The Ceausescu trial was a travesty of justice: The defense lawyers acted like a second prosecution, and there was no appeal and no request for clemency. The entire period from arrest to execution lasted three days. A small number of top National Salvation Front leaders apparently decided on the death sentences on December 24, 1989, before the trial had even started.

Moreover, the Ceausescu trial could not have constituted a true settling of accounts where there is a public disclosure of the facts coupled with a reasoned, normative judgment. The trial was not public, as had been originally promised, and there was no opportunity for a full airing of the wrongs committed by the Ceausescu regime. Equally important, the trial failed to elucidate what had caused the switch from street violence on the evening of December 21, 1989 to a jubilant celebration with Army backing the next morning. Finally, as the first major public act of the provisional government, the trial did nothing to fulfil the new regime's stated goals of moving toward a rule-of-law state with a democratic order. On the contrary, the trial tarnished the image of the new regime in international public opinion, with the executions uniformly criticized by foreign governments and international human rights groups.

More Trials

The Ceausescu trial was just the first of many trials. Although none of the later trials demonstrated as egregious a disregard of fair judicial procedures, they were nonetheless responsible for undermining public confidence in the judiciary. Trumped-up charges and then later releases on contrived grounds neither elucidated the historical record nor provided any indication that decisions were grounded in principle.

The machinery of justice began with an emphasis on the prosecution of so-called terrorists that ultimately came to nothing. Extraordinary military tribunals were set up in each of the forty-one Romanian counties and Bucharest according to a decree-law published on January 8, 1990. They were empowered to use the summary procedures employed for offenses *in flagrante delicto* and to try criminal offenses which were committed with a view to suppressing the people's revolution and destabilizing the state, threatening its very existence and the life, physical integrity and health of persons, the public and personal patrimony and the assets of the national cultural patrimony.

The very existence of terrorists was later doubted, however, especially after some time had passed and none of the supposed scores of terrorists were brought to justice.

A number of highly publicized trials, however, did take place in the aftermath of Ceausescu's fall from power. The first of them, commencing on January 27, 1990, concerned Ceausescu's four closest aides: former minister of the interior Tudor Postelnicu, former deputy premier Ion Dinca, former Communist Party Organization chief Emil Bobu, and former first deputy premier Manea Manescu. In a well-publicized show trial with rehearsed, self-critical testimony, which the defendants later renounced, the four pleaded guilty to complicity in genocide for their role in issuing orders to fire on demonstrators in December 1989. All four were sentenced to life imprisonment, and all of their property was confiscated. Soon after, in March 1990, proceedings that came to be known as the Timisoara trial charged more than two dozen Securitate and police officers with complicity in genocide for the killings in Timisoara and the secret removal of corpses to Bucharest for burning. Subject to numerous delays, the trial lasted nearly two years, with over 500 witnesses having been heard. Charges were eventually modified to aggravated murder and complicity in murder. When the verdict was read on December 9, 1991 eight defendants were jailed, with sentences ranging from fifteen to twenty-five years. Six of the remaining defendants were acquitted, one died, and ten others were convicted but were pardoned or released when the time served during the investigation and trial was taken into account.

In April 1993, however, the Supreme Court reconsidered the case of Ceausescu's four closest advisers and commuted the charges from complicity in genocide to aggravated manslaughter and complicity in aggravated manslaughter, reducing the sentences to between ten and seventeen years. By 1994, all four had been released, benefiting from medical releases or a parole procedure that commutes three quarters to two thirds of a jail term for anyone over the age of sixty. All of those convicted in the Timisoara trial had also been released on health grounds. Each of the releases, gradually announced over the course of many months, was marked by little more than a small press notice.

Another group trial centering around the events of December 1989 involved the entire Political Executive Committee of the Romanian Communist Party (other than the four persons charged in January) and started in July 1990. The procedural history of this case provides perhaps the most telling example of the arbitrary justice meted out in these trials. The members of the committee were originally charged with genocide for approving Ceausescu's orders to fire on demonstrators in Timisoara on December 17, 1989 and in Bucharest on December 21, 1989. The military prosecutor later reduced the charge to instigation to aggravated murder. In March 1991, the military court of first instance convicted nine of the members on charges it further reduced to complicity in murder and negligence of duty. The rest were acquitted or received suspended sentences. The convictions were overturned on appeal in December 1991, but the general prosecutor launched an extraordinary appeal to the civilian section of the Supreme Court. The result was that all twenty-one defendants were convicted in a final judgment on new charges of complicity in aggravated murder and attempted complicity in aggravated murder. Yet in the end, three of the defendants are officially on parole, and the others have been released for health reasons.

Ceausescu family members, many of whom held public positions, were also brought up on charges. Most notable, the notorious younger son of the ruling couple, Nicu Ceausescu, was prosecuted for ordering the shooting of demonstrators in December 1989 in the Transylvanian city of Sibiu, where he was the local first secretary of the Communist Party. N. Andruta Ceausescu, a brother of Nicolae Ceausescu and a former Securitate lieutenant-general, was sentenced to fifteen years for aggravated murder, complicity in murder, and firearms violations for his role in the violence on December 21-22, 1989, including having personally shot seven people. Other family members, including the two other Ceausescu children, were investigated or charged with the undermining of the state economy, embezzlement, or fraud.

But even son Nicu Ceausescu rode the ups and downs of a seemingly ambivalent judiciary. He was originally sentenced to twenty years for genocide. Appeals filed in his case first reduced the charges against him to instigation to aggravated murder and illegal possession of firearms and later reinstated the genocide charge. In the end, the only charge that stuck was the illegal possession of firearms, carrying a five-year jail term. Nicu served only half of that sentence, however; he was paroled, partly for health reasons, in November 1992. His release received little public attention. One newspaper account quoted a shopkeeper's reaction: "People are so worried about where they can get food and if they will lose their jobs. They do not have time to bother about the fact that it is unjust for him to be released. There are too many other problems. Winter is here and we are cold." Brother Andruta Ceausescu, currently out of jail, has also quietly benefited from at least two temporary releases from prison on medical grounds.

These trials differed significantly from the Ceausescus' trial in that they were held before the regular military courts, and many of the sessions were broadcast live on television, with journalists welcome to attend the sessions. In addition, the death penalty had been abolished on the day after Christmas, giving Elena and Nicolae Ceausescu the distinction of being the executioner's last two victims. Nevertheless, the later trials, too, contributed to the impression that a highly politicized judiciary was implementing a purge of the top leadership at least as much as it was accounting for human rights abuses. That impression was aggravated by the lack of a clear underlying theory of prosecution and the conflation of human rights prosecutions with investigations into the financial dealings of the Ceausescu children. In addition, trying most of the defendants in large groups contributed to confusing guilt by job title with individualized responsibility. In the end, the subtlety of the accusations against the Political Executive Committee, whether its members were criminally culpable for acquiescing in Ceausescu's decision to fire on demonstrators, was undoubtedly lost on the general Romanian public.

At the same time, the gradual reduction of charges and suspiciously consistent parole and medical release practices have resulted in an apparent failure to hold anyone responsible other than Nicolae and Elena Ceausescu. The post-Ceausescu trials present the worst aspects of two contradictory political impulses. They started as highly politicized show trials caught up in the hysteria of the moment, but in the end the concrete results were effectively subverted through indirect means, presumably due to political influence. The main result has been a further erosion of public confidence in the rule of law; with it, any deterrence value of the trials has been undermined.

Ambiguous "Amnesties"

On the heels of the revolution, on January 4, 1990, Ion Iliescu, acting as the president of the National Salvation Front Council, announced a general amnesty for political offenses committed from December 30, 1947 until December 22, 1989. Political offenses were defined in article one of the decree as deeds that had as their purpose:

a. protest against dictatorship, the cult of personality, terror or the abuse of power by the authorities;
b. the respect of fundamental human rights and freedoms, exercising civil, political, economic, social and cultural rights, or abolishing of discriminatory practices;
c. the satisfaction of democratic claims.

In addition, article two provided a general amnesty for any crime subject to a sentence of up to three years. Likewise, article three commuted any sentences of up to three years currently being served. The amnesty's cutoff date of December 22, 1989 was apparently intended to ensure that the so-called terrorists would not benefit from its provisions, but more significantly, the amnesty did include the key period leading up to Ceausescu's fall.

Ten days later, on January 15, 1990, Bucharest Radio reported that the National Salvation Front Council had issued a second decree-law, this time characterized as a pardon, but not limited to political offenses. Like the previously announced amnesty, the decree clearly provided that it would not benefit those convicted of murder, severe bodily injury, rape, theft, and prison escape as well as abuse of power contrary to the public interest, bribery, intercession, illegal arrest and abusive investigation, ill-treatment and unfair repression. Unlike the previously announced amnesty, however, the decree also provided that it would not benefit:

> *The individuals who, having participated in the leadership or service of the old dictatorial regime, actively suppressing human rights and freedoms or carrying out other of the objectives of that regime, or simply acting within it in the service of their own interest or in order to avoid responsibility, perpetrated crimes against peace and humanity, or against the state, as well as crimes of illegal arrest, abuse on duty, violation of arms regulations., terrorist acts or complicity in terrorist acts.*

Although the January 15 pardon appears to be carefully limited so as not to cover any human rights abuses, the prior general amnesty which did not contain the same qualifications still holds for crimes subject to sentences of three years or less. The ambiguous relationship of the two decrees was never explained to the general public; indeed, few people are aware that two different decrees existed. Moreover, all political prisoners were released immediately after Ceausescu's departure, before either decree was announced.

The full benefits of the January 4 amnesty decree became clearer when Securitate officers and other former officials began to benefit from its provisions. For example, in March 1991, five Securitate high officers were convicted for "unlawful deprivation of liberty" under article 189 of the criminal code for detaining Dumitru Mazilu and his family from December 21 to December 22, 1989. Mazilu, a one-time Securitate officer himself, was a former U.N. diplomat turned dissident who later participated in the formation of the National Salvation Front.

Although seemingly appropriate, the officers were not charged under article 266 of the criminal code, which prohibits "illegal arrest and abusive investigation" and is excluded by the general amnesty. As a result, Emil Radulescu and Gheorghe Manea, sentenced to two and a half years each, were amnestied according to the January 4 decree-law. Defendants in the Timisoara trial and other trials concerning the events of December 1989 also benefited from the decree.

In the end, then, the popular move of providing an amnesty for offenses of political protest provided a vehicle for simultaneously forgiving human rights abuses with little attention. Indeed, the restrictions contained in the later pardon misleadingly gave the impression that no human rights abuses would go unpunished.

Nonetheless, the decrees do leave room for the prosecutions of many persons who would have committed human rights abuses under the authority of the Communist regime, at least if they committed crimes subject to a sentence of more than three years. Indeed, the pardon refers, in part, to the exclusion of "crimes against peace" and "crimes against humanity" that were established by the Nuremberg courts after World War II. The opportunity they provide, however, has not been seized.

Confronting the Communist Regime

Like the summary trial of the Ceausescus, the morally evocative charge of genocide initially leveled at most of the post-Ceausescu defendants served to deflect much of the newly awakened public outrage at decades of victimization. Genocide does not, however, refer merely to large-scale killings, as the Romanian authorities and media implied at the time. Genocide has a specific meaning under international law, which is mirrored in the Romanian Penal Code. It requires an intent to destroy, in whole or in part, a national, ethnic, racial, or religious group (as such). The only group distinction shared by the victims of state violence in December 1989 was a political one, making a genocide claim incompatible with international law. Indeed, the genocide charges were, for the most part, ultimately dropped, especially when it became clear that the numbers of dead and wounded during December 1989 had been exaggerated.

But the misuse of the genocide charge superficially masked a more important omission. The charges in the 1990 trials were exclusively limited to the "events of December." There was no investigation or prosecution relating to the political persecutions of the Ceausescu years, for which many of the same defendants arguably were responsible. Moreover, the abuses of the harsh, Stalinist regime of Ceausescu's predecessor, Gheorghiu-Dej, which included mass deportations, extrajudicial executions, disappearances, political arrests, torture, and forced labour, were not mentioned.

Even before the 1990 trials were under way, well-known dissident Doina Cornea spoke of her concerns: "It is impossible to judge people only on what they did on the day the revolution started. Everybody must be judged by the people. I am not in favor of vengeance, I have always advocated human rights. But you cannot pass the death sentence on a couple and say that everything else is fine." Once the trials began, critics like Octavian Paler, an intellectual writing for the newly formed independent newspaper *Romania Libera*, advocated strongly for a more comprehensive approach to the trials: "Does justice want that these trials be limited, that they should not accuse the Communist system? Why? Does it believe that the massacre in Timisoara can be understood by avoiding the roots of the evil which lie in the totalitarian order?"

By the time the one-year anniversary of December 1989 came around, the government was at least superficially acknowledging the problem. In what may have been an early sign of an impending split between the president and the more reform-minded prime minister Petre Roman, the justice minister, speaking on Roman's behalf, issued a stem public criticism of the prosecutor's office:

The penal bodies, more particularly the prosecutor's office, are in duty bound to take each case separately and establish one's contribution to the country's disaster and to the attempt to repress the revolution, and bring the culprits to court because they are to be held responsible for what they have done against the country and the Romanian people for more than forty years, including the hot revolution days when they shot at an unarmed population. To conceal the truth and to procrastinate the moment of doing justice means to work against the Romanian people's interests of today and tomorrow, and that is why the passive attitude of the penal bodies, of the prosecutor's office, can no longer be tolerated.

The statement concluded that "the country's rebirth, national reconciliation and the restitution of Romania's true image to the rest of the world" could not be achieved without prosecutions. The prosecutor's office reacted defensively, citing the thousands of depositions, expert appraisals, searches, and other inquiries that had been necessary merely to indict those responsible for the repression in December 1989. "The prosecutors are doing all they can to find out the truth and punish those guilty of crimes against the Romanian people," their official response insisted. But the exchange of public statements ultimately proved to be mere window dressing, because no new criminal investigations were initiated.

By the end of 1991, pressure began to mount on the prosecutor's office to initiate a "trial of communism" that would address the human rights abuses of the Communist regime. The Association of Former Political Prisoners filed a formal complaint regarding crimes committed under communism, and there were a series of meetings between the justice ministry, the prosecutor's office, and leaders of several civic organizations, such as the Association of Former Political Prisoners, the League for the Defense of Human Rights, the Romanian Helsinki Committee, and the December 21 Association. Negotiations continued for about eight months. The nongovernmental organizations wanted to start by making examples of the most notorious figures from the Stalinist period of 1946 to 1964, such as Teoharie Georgescu, Alexandru Nicolski, and Alexandru Draghici. Georgescu was responsible for operating a prison in Pitesti and devising the "Pitesti phenomenon," a particularly brutal psychological and physical torture process that resulted in the conversion of the torture victims themselves into torturers. Nicolski was the chief of the Securitate under Gheorghiu-Dej, and Draghici was the minister of the interior, responsible for signing the orders for the internal displacement of tens of thousands and sending untold thousands, including political prisoners who had served their sentences, to forced labour camps near the Black Sea where they helped dig the Danube canal. Many died in the camps from the ill-treatment and hard conditions. In total, Nicolski and Draghici were responsible for the arrest and detention of at least hundreds of thousands of political prisoners, according to estimates by the Association of Former Political Prisoners and others.

The discussions with the prosecutor's office proved futile and broke off. Georgescu had been long dead, and Nicolski died of a heart attack around the same time an arrest warrant was issued. No action was taken against Draghici until after he fled to Hungary. Finally, in August 1992, the prosecutor's office issued an arrest warrant and sought Draghici's extradition for ordering the 1954 murder of a Turkish citizen following a dispute in a café.

Hungarian authorities balked at the request for extradition in early 1993 because the Hungarian proscriptive period for murder, thirty years, had expired. The Romanian-Hungarian Treaty of Mutual Juridical Assistance stipulates, in relevant part: "Extradition shall not take place if, according to the laws of the side to whom the application was submitted, the penal action cannot be carried out owing to the prescription terms having been reached or other legal grounds." Romanian authorities argued, nevertheless, that bringing any high officials before justice was unthinkable under the Communist regime, thus constituting a *force majeure* and suspending the running of the prescriptive period.

Unable to convince the Hungarian authorities, the prosecutor's office went forward in May 1993 and prosecuted Draghici in absentia along with three Securitate aides who had been involved in the killing. The prosecution relied in large part on documentation provided by the Romanian Intelligence Service, the successor to the Securitate, based on a 1968 investigation. By March 1994, however, Draghici had died. On March 19, 1994 the Military Section of the Supreme Court in Bucharest issued an order of no indictment for all four defendants based on the passing of the prescriptive period.

In April 1993, another prosecution for abuses committed under the Communist regime commenced. Tudor Postelnicu, who was in prison at the time for his role in the events of December 1989, and George Homosteanu, another former minister of the Interior, were charged along with seven Securitate officers. They were accused of carrying out Ceausescu's orders for the summary execution of three people who attempted to highjack a bus to the West in 1981. Two of the three Securitate officers accused of carrying out the killing admitted their guilt. In July 1993, the Bucharest Military Tribunal convicted all nine, handing down sentences of up to eighteen years. Yet along with the others involved in the trial of Ceausescu's four closest advisers described earlier, Postelnicu remains free nonetheless.

These token prosecutions, which have had only a very limited success, represent a tiny fraction of the potential cases. Indeed, out of frustration over less than vigorous official efforts, nongovernmental groups have attempted to launch prosecutions by doing their own fact finding. To date the prosecutor's office has accepted for consideration four cases based on information provided by the League for the Defense of Human Rights. One case documented the extrajudicial execution of three men near Targu Mures who were arrested in 1948. In July 1993, the Targu Mures prosecutor exhumed the three skeletons and found that each had been shot in the skull. Nevertheless, bringing the case to trial is difficult because the identities of the officials responsible are not known. Generally, the ability of human rights groups or other nongovernmental organizations to establish enough of a factual basis for further prosecutions is hampered by a 1991 decision by the Romanian parliament to seal Securitate records for forty years.

In addition to prosecuting the systematic gross violations of human rights that were especially prevalent before Ceausescu took power, some Romanians urge that the scope of a trial of communism include some of the subtler abuses of the Ceausescu regime. Indeed, as former dissidents and others contend, many Ceausescu policies caused widespread suffering and abused the rights of millions of Romanians. For instance, Ceausescu's "systemization" policy resulted in the bulldozing of entire villages. Urban planning policies resulted in the razing of entire sections of Bucharest, including many historic churches and other buildings of historical or architectural significance. Demographic policies under the Ceausescu regime criminalized abortions and financially penalized childless women and men over twenty-five years of age. Doctors faced criminal sentences if they failed to inform the prosecutor's office of emergency medical procedures meaning that many women died from unattended complications rather than confess to an illegal abortion. Economic policies that subsidized the development of a large but substandard industry and ignored Romania's rich agricultural resources arguably caused unnecessary misery for most Romanian citizens, who suffered through food shortages and winters without heat. Uncommonly widespread and intrusive surveillance created a climate heavy with fear and intimidation.

Some Romanians argue that decision makers for such policies should be held accountable along with those responsible for authorizing or carrying out extrajudicial executions, torture, and other gross violations of human rights. As atrocious as the policies were, however, determining individual criminal responsibility for devising the policies would not be an easy task. Prosecutors would face an enormous line-drawing problem since the scope of complicity could be potentially enormous. Romanian laws currently on the books that punish crimes such as "hostile actions toward the state" or "undermining the state economy" could probably be invoked. But using excessively vague criminal provisions of the prior regime would not contribute to the creation of a rule-of-law state. Trying crimes that easily lend themselves to political interpretation could, in fact, be a dangerous precedent and would not help to depoliticize the judiciary.

Regardless of the scope of a trial of communism, proponents of such a trial argue that its value is fundamental to the political tranformation currently underway in Romania. Constantin Ticu Dumitrescu, the president of the Association of Former Political Prisoners and an opposition senator in the Romanian parliament has written:

The trial of communism, in its correct and complete sense, pursues restoration of the historic truth, the recuperation of the memory of our past, of the sense of social justice, with a view to the moral curing and civil and political emancipation of our people. The trial of communism is, in fact, a condition of democratization, the Romanian revolution's last chance.

Gabriel Andreescu, founder of the Civic Alliance and president of the Romanian Helsinki Committee, adds that from a juridical point of view, a trial of communism must concern itself with individual responsibility for particular crimes. But the *force majeure* justification for the suspension of the prescriptive period, that the very existence of the Communist regime prevented such prosecutions, refers to a collective event. It is in this sense, says Andreescu, that a trial of communism can be thought about collectively without sacrificing the principle of individual responsibility.

Although no trial of communism has taken place and

there have been only a very few efforts to prosecute any human rights abuses of the Communist regime compensation for human rights victims has been addressed relatively swiftly. The Association for Former Political Prisoners was formed at the beginning of January 1990 with the express purpose of seeking reparations for the suffering of its members. Its efforts were successful, and law 118/90, passed in early 1990, provided a supplementary pension of 200 lei a month for every year persons persecuted by the Communist regime served in a prison or forced labour camp. Applicants must provide a ministry of the interior certificate proving they were detained for political reasons.

The government also announced that it would offer moral compensation by inscribing former political prisoners' names in a list to be known as the White Book. As of 1994, however, publication was withheld because the Association of Former Political Prisoners complained that the list was misleading. Containing 37,000 names, the list covered only three detention sites, a small fraction of the total number. Indeed, when the Association formed in 1990, more than double that number of former political prisoners registered with the organization. The Romanian Intelligence Service, in a 1993 report to parliament, claimed to have processed more than 70,000 applications for "moral compensation and due rights" by victims of political repression. Also in 1993, the parliament passed a law rehabilitating judges who had been fired for political reasons after the Communists took power. For more recent victims, "revolutionary certificates" were awarded to those who fought in the revolution, were wounded in it, or had a relative who was killed in it. The certificates entitle their holders to tax breaks.

Decommunization

A trial of communism represents perhaps the most extreme measure available to punish human rights abuses committed under the Communist regime, and other Central and

Eastern European countries have generally avoided criminal proceedings in favour of vetting government officials and reforming institutions. Yet Romania is unique in some respects. On the one hand, the Communist regime in Romania was one of the most repressive regimes in the region. On the other hand, with four million members in a country of twenty-three million people, the Romanian Communist Party had the highest per capita membership. As a result, there are strong political forces in Romania that both demand and resist decommunization.

When the National Salvation Front first announced its intention to provide provisional leadership as the country made a transition to a pluralistic, democratic system, its legitimacy was supported by a wide range of political actors, including several well-known dissidents, who became members. By the end of January 1990, however, the dissidents had abandoned the National Salvation Front and were accusing it of perpetuating the firm grip on power by elements from the old regime. Historical opposition parties from the interwar period had reformed and began to gain in strength. Despite the lack of a tradition of organized dissident groups like Charter 77 in Czechoslovakia or Solidarity in Polland, civic organizations began to form outside of the party process. One of them, the Timisoara Society, elaborated a statement enumerating demands that were believed necessary for the creation of a new democratic society. On March 11, 1990, workers' and students' associations gathered in Timisoara and adopted the thirteen-point "Timisoara Proclamation," which became the most coherent reflection of the popular sentiment that had moved the population to take to the streets in December. Point 7 of the Timisoara Proclamation questioned the role of the National Salvation Front: "Timisoara started the revolution against the entire Communist regime and its entire *nomenklatura*, and certainly not in order to give an opportunity to a group of anti-Ceausescu dissidents with the PCR [Romanian Communist Party] to take over the reins of political power." Point 8 provided that all former Communist activists and Securitate officers should be barred from running for public office, nationally and locally, for three consecutive legislatures. It also singled out the office of the president, opposing the right of those who had served the Communist regime as party activists, not as simple members to lead the country. The proclamation was immediately adopted by hundreds of independent associations, and nearly four million individuals registered their support over the next two months for incorporating point 8 into the election law. Nonetheless, the organizers of the 1990 elections pointedly ignored point 8, which would have excluded most of the leadership of the National Salvation Front, including its candidate for president, from running for office.

Point 8 of the Timisoara Proclamation also became a rallying cry during a massive demonstration at University Square on April 22, 1990 that turned into a marathon sit-in that blocked traffic in the center of Bucharest for months. The peaceful demonstration, which drew participants from a wide range of Romanian society, carried on through the first post-Ceausescu elections and ended in the violence of the "Mineriad" in June 1990. Iliescu's public reaction was to call the demonstrators tramps (*golani*) and charge them with attacking the majority of citizens, who had been linked to communism through party membership of themselves or family members: "People try to identify all of the evils of the old regime with the members of the Communist Party. But this can turn into a dangerous witch hunt." The leaders of the demonstration insisted that they were not interested in punishment, only in having party activists "stop claiming that they represent us."

After Iliescu won the May elections, the demonstration dwindled in size. At dawn on June 13, 1990, the police moved in, beating and arresting many of the protestors. Protestors retaliated throughout the day. After President Iliescu made a public appeal that evening, the miners from the Jiu Valley east of Bucharest arrived the next day to restore order. The events that ensued, known as the Mineriad in Romania, have become the blackest spot in the history of the new regime. Hundreds of demonstrators and others in the street were beaten, and at least a dozen or so were killed. Violence spread as miners went after targeted personalities, and opposition party headquarters were ransacked. The events ended in a pogrom against Gypsies (*Roma*) in a neighbourhood of Bucharest with a large Roma population. By June 15, when the miners left, the public that had been demonstrating for months in University Square lost any hope that their message would be heard by those in power.

But the Mineriad stands for more than just the end of dialogue with the ruling government. There has never been a public acknowledgement of responsibility by the government for the miners' violence. A parliamentary commission designated to investigate the events issued two contradictory reports, one authored by the National Salvation Front (the majority) and the other authored by opposition parties (the minority). Despite complaints filed with the prosecutor's office by human rights groups and others, no one has been prosecuted. Thus, June 1990 confirmed the pattern that had been developing in the trials that followed the fall of Ceausescu. It was a pattern that would be mirrored again and again when vigilante mobs torched Roma homes in dozens of villages in Romania, police beat or tortured prisoners, and miners descended on Bucharest in another bloody confrontation in September 1991. One argument in favour of prosecuting past human rights abuses is that leaving the abuses unpunished invites repetition, and the post- Ceausescu record in Romania provides ample support for it. When asked whether there was any guarantee against a future repetition of June 1990 and other violent episodes, one human rights activist responded, "We have hopes, but the only guarantee would be to punish those responsible."

Establishing the Truth

One prime motivation of the advocates of a trial of communism was simply to establish the truth of what happened under the Communist regime. Moreover, the most egregious of the human rights abuses committed under the Communist regime took place decades ago, and many of the persons responsible for it are dead. As Constantin Ticu Dumitrescu, president of the Association of Former Political Prisoners, acknowledges, "Our purpose is not revenge or punishment because we have no one to punish. All we want is the truth." Opposition senator Alexandru Paleologu, who served time as a political prisoner during the Gheorghiu-Dej regime and was the first post-Ceausescu ambassador to France, emphasizes the wide implications: "The past cannot be forgotten because a society with amnesia is a primitive society. In a true society, there is a collective memory and a law and an agenda for those elected."

There have been efforts to establish the truth without resorting to criminal proceedings. A draft law that would allow individuals to see their own secret police files was introduced in December 1993 and then modified in July 1994, but does not appear to be very high on the legislative agenda. Nevertheless, even without access to the secret police files, a powerful and moving series of television documentaries initiated in late 1990, *Memorial of Pain*, has been able to clarify many of the human rights issues of the past through oral history. The twenty-fourth episode, broadcast in July 1993, for example, interviewed former political prisoners who had been arrested in a crackdown on dissidents and protest organizers who had been inspired by the 1956 Hungarian uprising. The series is extremely popular, and as one of the only sources of credible information, each episode becomes a point of reference for anyone interested in the human rights abuses committed under communism. Books have also been published, for instance, one on the Pitesti phenomenon and another presenting the notebooks of a *Memorial of Pain* subject. Periodical sources containing primary documents and analytical articles also became popular after the revolution but are less widely read than they once were. A new history textbook with a revised discussion of the Communist regime was announced in the spring of 1993.

New museums have been established, too. In the early fall of 1992, as an election campaign was under way, one of the destroyed buildings on "Revolution Square," where Ceausescu gave his last speech, was transformed into a Museum of the Resistance at the initiative of the Civic Alliance. For its first exhibit, the burntout shell of the red brick building formerly housing the Fifth Division of the Securitate was draped with three-story-long sheets containing the names of political prisoners who died in Romanian prisons under the Communist regime. In addition, a Museum of Totalitarianism was announced in the spring of 1993, to be established in Sighet, one of the most notorious penitentiaries for political prisoners in northwest Romania.

Nevertheless, rediscovering history has been difficult, even for relatively recent events. The Romanian senate finally established a commission to investigate the events of December 1989 in early 1991, but the commission did not hear its first witnesses until the summer of 1993. Although a December 1993 deadline was set for the commission's report, the senate postponed the due date by an additional year in November 1993. In the meantime, Senator Dumitrescu had resigned as chairman of the commission in protest over the lack of cooperation from state authorities. In addition, a senate commission to investigate the miners' attacks in September 1991 has not yet presented its long overdue findings. The majority and minority reports issued by the commission investigating the events of June 1990 merely emphasized how politicized the official truth-seeking process was.

Romania had an especially intense experience with the

manipulation of information for political purposes under communism. As Senator Alexandru Paleologu, Romania's ambassador to France in 1990, put it: "What was true was what you *said*, not what 'is.' There was an official version of the truth. Even after 1989, there was a reflex people were not accustomed to discussing the truth." The manipulative techniques of official elites are imitated throughout society, according to Paleologu, sometimes causing popular reactions that are equally uninformative.

In the context of impunity for past human rights abuses, the "truth" about the past must consist of information concerning who were the victims of abuses, what happened to them, and who was responsible for the abuses. In addition, such information should be accompanied by some sort of official acknowledgment. In Romania, however, the "truth" often consists of a series of politicized conclusions, without much discussion of the underlying facts. Sometime the "truth" is merely obfuscation or mystification. Even for those operating in good faith, the end result is preaching to the choir without the satisfaction of universal acknowledgment.

Summary

Generally, countries in transition are faced with choices about how to address past human rights abuses. Options generally include criminal prosecution, vetting of officials and institutional reform, compensation of victims, and investigation and creation of an historical record. But the issues that most of those choices raise have barely been addressed in Romania, mainly because of a general perception that there is no choice. Proponents of criminal proceedings have been stymied, and there appears to be little hope of a satisfactory official investigation and accounting for past abuses, or for more recent ones. Yet Romania may be a paradigm case of a country struggling with reactionary forces but eager for international approval. In the early 1990s, two of the most important foreign policy issues, for instance, have been the restoration of most-favored-nation trade status by the United States and admission to the Council of Europe, both of which have subjected Romania to a thorough scrutiny of its human rights record. In addition, it is posited that a solid basis in international law is necessary to avoid the appearance of mere "political vengeance." Yet the prosecutions that have taken place to date in Romania do seem to have more in common with political vengeance than with accountability.

If international legal obligations to investigate and prosecute serious human rights violations had clearer political consequences, perhaps Romanian authorities would have taken greater measures to end the cycle of impunity. But regardless of any international political consequences, the most important factor preventing Romania from confronting its past has been its strange hybrid transition. Despite diplomatic pressure to investigate or prosecute abuses, the political will necessary to ensure that such obligations are carried out in good faith has been lacking.

The impunity enjoyed by the Communist regime appears to pertain with equal force to the recent past, with profound implications for the Romanian present and future. Although the passage of time and a history of frustrated hopes have decreased demands for a public accounting, the largely unresolved trauma of the Communist regime and the murkiness of the "revolution" and its aftereffects continue to spawn mistrust. One important consequence is that the Romanian public has failed to regain confidence in the rule of law. Indeed, Romanians often regard seeking a remedy for a human rights violation through the courts as a futile gesture. Thus, the persistent culture of impunity has significantly impeded the project of establishing a stable democratic order.

8

Blaming and Punishing Individuals for Human Rights Violations

Introduction

A nation seeking to rectify past governmental wrong by applying the rule of law encounters particular tensions. The rule of law may rival the sense of justice: Protective procedural guarantees present obstacles to punishing persons responsible for human rights violations who went unprosecuted under the former government or state. Another impediment to the mastering of the past (*Vergangenheitsbewältigung*) is that the law, particularly the criminal law, was designed with classical, not governmental, criminality in mind. Governmental criminality, with its links to the political and societal dogmas of an entire government and legal system and to the world political scene, may well be beyond the reach of the criminal law.

These links generate problems regarding not only the scope of the criminal law but also the function of the judiciary. Can it remain true to its judicial function and avoid the appearance of political trials? Can law and justice on the one hand and political morality and legitimacy on the other be neatly separated? Altogether, the *Vergangenheitsbewältigung* after German reunification is so complex that we are faced with a dilemma. Should we approach the German Democratic Republic (GDR) case as we would any other with our set of analytic tools derived from West German experience? By doing so, do we run the risk of a kind of local bias? Questions like these do not lend themselves to easy answers and perhaps ultimately cannot be solved at a national level.

Nevertheless, the occurrence of grave human rights violations in the GDR is undisputed, and focusing on these violations is within the legitimate function of the criminal courts. The unique situation in Germany arises because the state whose past is at issue dissolved voluntarily and joined the Federal Republic by way of consensual treaty. This creates the awkward situation that one party to the treaty has assumed the position of judge over the past of the other. The absence of an explicit stipulation of jurisdiction in the reunification treaty itself, particularly with respect to the responsibility of leading state officials for acts of state, gives rise to the suspicion that the stronger party is subduing the defeated.

Criminal prosecution of grave human rights violations is now in progress. The term "*Regierungskriminalität*" ("government criminality") encompasses a number of vastly different, wrongful acts of state (or acts attributable to the state). State Security Service (Stasi) repression of critics and opponents of the regime, activities that are still under investigation, may turn out to be the most egregious forms. At first, however, the focus of criminal prosecution was on the trials of GDR border soldiers accused of killing East German citizens who attempted illegally to cross the border into the West, particularly at the Berlin Wall. The Berlin Wall shootings will likely not prove among the gravest violations of human rights. They are, however, not only among the most visible; more important, perhaps, these cases allow us to single out immediately individuals who are *prima facie* responsible for them the low-level soldiers who pulled the trigger.

The *Vergangenheitsbewältigung* is not limited to criminal prosecution but encompasses other forms of legal redress as well. Among the most important of these is the review of GDR convictions. Judicial powers of redress include cassation (annulment) and the authority to award compensation for wrongful prosecution, retrial, a declaration of incompatibility with rule of law standards or inappropriateness of legal consequence, and rehabilitation of persons convicted for making use of their basic political rights. Other forms of redress include legislative efforts toward compensation for the victims of the SED regime, as well as the unprecedented opening of the Stasi documents. Each area raises its own set of questions. In this chapter, I shall cast some light on the problems of criminal prosecution as exemplified by the Berlin Wall cases. While in the meantime, more cases involving killings at the Wall have been tried and reviewed, the focus of this chapter is on the Bundesgerichtshof's first appellate opinion reviewing the criminal responsibility of the border soldiers (*Mauerschützen* I); I also address the high court's opinion reviewing the manslaughter convictions of high-level political leaders in the so-called Honecker case.

First I briefly outline the relevant post unification criminal law issues and then discuss the international and constitutional law issues the courts had to face in establishing the border soldiers' criminal responsibility. A look at problems of individual attribution and personal culpability is followed by a consideration of the special problems in trying Honecker and other top-level officials. I then discuss the problems of sentencing in the *Mauerschützen* cases and raise the issue of appropriate sanctions in human rights cases in general. I conclude with some perspectives on the legitimacy of *ex post facto* criminal justice and on the problems of state prosecution of human rights cases in general.

Postunification Criminal Law Issues

Between the construction of the Berlin Wall in August 1961 and its destruction in November 1989, over 200 people were killed by GDR soldiers at the inter-German border. The last death occurred just a few months before the Wall fell. In reunified Germany prosecutors began the process of determining who, if anyone, can be held criminally responsible for these killings.

Homicide investigations against border soldiers initiated prior to October 3, 1990 by the General Prosecutor of the GDR were taken over by prosecutors at the Landgericht Berlin according to the regulations of the Unification Treaty. The first case against border soldiers, *Mauerschützen I*, which implicated four defendants, arose out of an attempt of two young GDR citizens to overcome the Wall not long before its fall. Defendant H., who was initially sentenced to three years, six months of imprisonment for manslaughter in a minor degree, had shot at a fugitive from a distance of less than 40 meters as he was about to overcome a metal fence, the last border security device on GDR ground. According to the judicial findings, after fruitlessly firing two warning shots, the defendant aimed at the fugitive's upper body and thereby took into account that his shot could be deadly. Defendant K., who was initially sentenced to two years on probation, had shot with automatic gunfire from his Kalaschnikow from a distance of at least 125 metres, which according to the Landgericht constituted attempted manslaughter. Two other defendants were acquitted. In the second case, *Mauerschützen II*, according to the judicial findings of fact as stipulated in the BGH's fifth senate appellate decision, defendant W. was a junior officer and H. a soldier in the GDR border troops. On December 1, 1984 at 3:15 A.M. they shot at twenty-year-old GDR citizen S., who was climbing a ladder and about to cross the Wall into West Berlin. Defendant W., after ordering S. to stop and after firing warning shots, fired at S. at a distance of approximately 150 meters, while defendant H. shot from a distance of 110 meters. Within five seconds each guard had fired more than twenty bullets. The bullet that caused the fugitive's death entered his back when he had already put his hand on the top of the wall. Although S. would have lived had he received immediate medical care, because of secrecy and regulations defining specific job duties, he was not taken to a hospital until more than two hours later and died there.

Both defendants testified that they did not want to kill S., whom they believed to be a spy, saboteur, or "criminal," but that they were aware of the possibility of a deadly hit. Before entering into service at the border they had been asked whether they were willing to shoot "border violators," which they answered in the affirmative. Before each turn standing guard they were subject to a "guard mount," which outlined the course of action to take in the event of a border violation; included was the possible use of deadly force if it was necessary to thwart flight.

The pivotal questions for the prosecution were what law to apply and whether the border soldiers accused of wilful homicide could claim grounds of justification or excuse. Under East German law, justification was conceivable based on the GDR's border law firearms provisions. If West German law applied, however, justification would be ruled out, leaving only the possibility of excuse based on unavoidable lack of consciousness of wrongdoing (mistake of law).

After 1973, West German courts generally applied West German law as far as provided by the rules of international jurisdiction when adjudicating crimes committed in the GDR. On the basis of the Unification Treaty, however, it is widely agreed that crimes committed in the GDR before October 3, 1990 must be analyzed twice: first according to the applicable laws of the GDR and then according to those of the unified Germany. The results are then compared and the more lenient law applied.

Under East German law, the use of firearms by border soldiers at the inter-German border was authorized under certain circumstances. Whether such circumstances included the use of deadly force to stop those unlawfully trying to leave or whether such shootings instead constituted criminal homicide became a crucial issue.

Neither the internal orders and regulations of the ministries for national defense and the interior regulating the use of firearms nor the border-security regulations in section 27 of the border law of 1982 authorized killing with intent or contingent intent. However, the internal regulations authorized the use of firearms if and when necessary to arrest persons disregarding the orders of border patrols, and the 1982 border law authorized the use of firearms "to prevent the imminent commission or continuation of a crime which under the circumstances constitutes a felony." The GDR Criminal Code had only to declare the "unlawful frontier-crossing" a felony, which it did for "grave cases": crossing the frontier with accomplices or crossing by way of "dangerous means and methods," for example, constituted grave cases justifying the use of firearms. According to the prevailing view, overcoming the high-security frontier fortifications practically always constituted a felony. Nonetheless, according to the letter of the law, the use of firearms had to be reasonable. Specifically, the use of firearms was defined as "the utmost measure of force against persons," with a person's life to be "spared as far as possible." Thus, the law of the GDR did not contain a literal statutory exemption for "contingently intentional" or reckless use of deadly force. And yet "to spare as far as possible" could justify killing the transgressor where the fleeing person could not otherwise be stopped. The LG Berlin, as well as the BSH, assumed this was the official GDR interpretation. It was repeatedly conveyed to the border soldiers during their routine guard mount; according to the judicial findings, the "*Befehlslage*" ("command status") for the thwarting of flight authorized even the conscious use of deadly force against fleeing persons if milder means were not sufficient.

International and Constitutional Law Problems of Establishing Criminal

If GDR law in *practice* permitted the use of deadly force against those fleeing over the Wall, the question becomes whether that law must now be accepted by the German courts, leading to acquittal. Acceptance of the justification provided by GDR law could be mandated by the notion that persons accused of crimes are protected by the principles of *nullum crimen sine lege* and *nullum crimen sine lege scripta*, principles laid down in the Federal Republic's Basic Law or Grundgesetz and in the European Convention for the Protection of Human Rights and Fundamental Freedoms (European Convention). Some authors therefore have cited the prohibition of retroactive establishment of criminal liability (*ex post facto* prohibition), encompassed by the *nullum crimen* principle, to support the view that justifications grounded in the GDR border law must be respected by the German courts today. According to this view, only "excessive perpetrators" those whose conduct went beyond the limits of the border law itself may be punished. For instance, if border soldiers shot at fleeing persons "with automatic machine-gun fire or with intent to kill," they can be punished. This was the view adopted by the LG Berlin in *Mauerschützen II*; the court held that the GDR border law was binding, but that the shootings in question had violated it. The BGH, on appeal, disagreed, finding that GDR state practice justified even the use of automatic machine gun fire and contingent (reckless) intent to kill to prevent border violations. Thus it needed to find another way to avoid the *ex post facto* problem.

Several doctrinal approaches are possible to avoid the *ex post facto* prohibition. First, the accusations could be elevated to the level of international crimes, as "crimes against humanity." The existence of international crimes of this kind was recognized in the statutes of the International Military Court at Nuremberg and at Tokyo and in Control Council Law No. 10. However, the use of firearms by individual border soldiers cannot be compared to the crimes adjudged crimes against humanity in Nuremberg and Tokyo.

Second, inalienable principles derived from natural law may override state granted impunity. As did our judiciary in trials of Nazi collaborators, the courts could rely on a "core of law, which according to universal conviction cannot be breached by any legislative act or any other authoritative measure." According to a leading judgment of the BGH in 1952, the "core of law" encompasses certain principles of human conduct, viewed as inviolable, which were built over time in all civilized peoples on the basis of commonly shared moral beliefs, and which remain legally binding even if particular provisions of the national legal systems seem to authorize their defiance.

The court conceded that it may be unclear where to draw the line; but in accordance with Radbruch's famous definition, it regarded it as transgressed where government orders do "not even aspire to justice, consciously deny the idea of equality, and clearly disregard the convictions, common to all cultured peoples, regarding the worth and dignity of the human person"; such orders "do not create law, and conduct in compliance with them remains Unrecht (un-law)." In another opinion the BGH had stated that assaults on life must be subject to particularly strict scrutiny: Except for the execution of a court-ordered death sentence, killings may be permissible only "if ensuing from an absolutely necessary use of force."

The LG Berlin in its first trial against border soldiers, citing this "core of law" jurisprudence, held that the *ex post facto* argument vitiates the principle that laws in violation of the core of law are null and void.

The legislature also may create Unrecht so that, if the practice of law is not to be left unarmed in the face of such conceivable historic developments, it must remain possible in extreme cases to value the principle of *Gerechtigkeit* (material justice) higher than the principle of *Rechtssicherheit* (certainty of the law), as generally represented by the validity of the written law.

In reviewing the LG's second conviction of border soldiers, the BGH, however, applied a third approach, which is doctrinally related but more concrete. The court did not base its decision on the "core of law" jurisprudence of the 1950s; in dicta, it called the application of "core of law" principles to cases of this kind "not easy, since the killing of human beings at the inter-German border cannot be put on an equal footing with the Nazi murder." Instead, the court relied on the GDR's own constitutional law in combination with international human rights law. It pointed out that the constitution of the GDR protected human life and that according to recognized doctrine, statutory limitations on this right were subject to scrutiny by a principle of reasonableness. Application of this standard had to include the consideration of human rights guarantees as laid down in international covenants binding on the GDR. The GDR had in 1974 ratified the International Covenant on Civil and Political Rights of 1966, and it entered into force in both German states in 1976. Since GDR state practice at the border violated the right to the protection of life and the right to leave, the border law could at no time be interpreted as a justification for the use of deadly force against unarmed fugitives.

By focusing on the "correct interpretation" of the border law as required by higher legal standards that had to be observed by the GDR, the court could overcome the hurdles posed by the *ex post facto* prohibition. The court recognized that the *ex post facto* prohibition protects not only against retroactive changes in the elements of a crime, but also of changes in the grounds of justification. However, since the letter of the border law (as interpreted in accordance with human rights guarantees) did not provide justification here, the defendants could only be shielded from prosecution if their actual reliance on state *practice* were encompassed by *ex post facto* protection. This the court did not accept; the expectation that the law will be *applied* in the future as it was at the time of conduct is not worthy of protection, where this would in effect lead to acceptance of justification grounds contrary to human rights.

The court's references to the right to the protection of life and the right to leave are, however, problematic. Although the GDR ratified the Covenant in 1974 and it entered into force in both German states in 1976, the GDR subsequently did not transform it into national law, as provided in article of the GDR Constitution. Arguably, without transformation the standards in the Covenant were not binding on the GDR. The BGH never directly addressed when the actual commitment to observance of rights guaranteed by the Covenant arose, assuming that ratification or promulgation made the Covenant internally binding even without transformation. Laudable as the court's elevation of international human rights over concerns of national sovereignty may be, the court largely ignored the international law problem of whether and when treaties are "self-executing." Instead, it was satisfied that the prevailing view in the GDR itself, as pronounced in an international law treatise, was that a state cannot avoid an international commitment by using its national legal order as a pretense. However, it is far from clear internationally if and when international human rights agreements take precedence over the lawmaking prerogative of sovereigns when it comes to the protection of the rights of the individual.

Moreover, a closer look reveals that the international consensus on the rights to the protection of life and to leave is less than airtight and that there are noticeable gray areas where protection of these rights conflicts with national security interests. As to the protection of life, it seems widely agreed that the use of firearms with *direct* intent to kill is in violation of article 6 of the Covenant, which protects against "arbitrary" deprivation of life. There seems to be no general consensus, however, on the limits of *possibly* deadly use of firearms that is, the lawful use of firearms where border officials are aware of the possibility of a deadly outcome.

As to the right to leave, international law guarantees leave something to be desired as well. The right is embodied in the Universal Declaration of Human Rights of December 10, 1948, as well as in numerous other human rights treaties, including article 12, clause 2 of the Covenant. Whether customary international law recognizes the right seems to be widely regarded as non verifiable. Again, neglecting the problems of transformation, the BGH held the GDR to its ratification and regarded its border system as a violation of the right to leave. The court considered the fact that "other states as well restrict their citizens' right to leave," that different opinions exist among members of the United Nations regarding the developing countries' desire to prevent the emigration of the intelligentsia, and that the authors of our own Basic Law did not want to embody the right to leave for fear of undesirable emigration of the working force. But the court believed the GDR practice distinguishable on at least two grounds: The denial of leave was the rule, not the exception, and the GDR border system was of "particular harshness." The court said:

Germans from the GDR [had] a special motive for their desire to cross the borders to West Berlin and West Germany: They and the people on the other side of the border belonged to one nation and were connected with them through manifold kinship and other personal relations. The situation created by the restrictive passport and leave regulations cannot be assessed under the aspect of human rights without regarding the real circumstances, characterized by the Wall, barbed wire, death zone and shooting order.

The court did not, however, examine the issue of travel restrictions enforced in the name of "national security," as upheld, for instance, in the *Elfes* judgment of the Federal Constitutional Court in 1957.

In sum, the court largely passed over the tremendous complexities regarding the historical background of East-West politics as well as thorny definitional problems regarding both the right to the protection of life and the right to leave.

Problems of Individual Attribution and Personal Culpability

The criminal law is concerned with the individual's culpability. The primary question is whether a given "result" is attributable to the alleged perpetrator or whether the role of the perpetrator was only that of aiding another person's crime. If one believes that the border soldiers were instruments of their superiors, one could argue that the actual perpetrators should be sought among the rear-rank commanders and decision makers and that the soldiers were mere aiders and abettors. In fact, under the strictly "subjective" theory that the BGH adopted thirty years ago, persons who had fulfilled all the elements for commission of a crime as principals could still be held responsible as accessories only, where, without their own crime interest, they merely executed the will of another. In the prosecutions of Nazi crimes at the time, application of this doctrine lead to the result that basically no one could be held as a principal for the most atrocious crimes. The highest-ups (who were dead) were deemed the "real" criminals, while those who had executed their will were regarded as accessories because they had acted without the requisite "interest" in bringing about the crime result. As part of the major criminal law reforms of the early seventies, the legislature ruled out such extreme results, particularly with regard to the responsibility of direct actors. Thus, today the BGH could address this point in routine fashion. The defendants had, acting in concert, fulfilled the elements of the crime; moreover, unlike persons who receive an order immediately before shooting, they also had a "certain room for action" because they were left on their own in case a fugitive suddenly appeared. This said, it can be deplored that the court passed over the historic chance to address directly the full dimension of complicity doctrine in cases of grave human rights violations.

Perhaps the biggest problem lies in the border soldiers' individual consciousness of wrongdoing. The LG Berlin as well as the BGH have adopted a rather rigorous view and rejected both the defenses of "action under superior orders" and of "mistake of law".

As to the defense of "superior orders," the BGH applied West German (military) law, the more lenient law, which exempts the subordinate from punishment except in cases where he recognizes that following an order would constitute unlawful action or where this is "obvious under the circumstances known to him." Interestingly, West German law recognizes no duty to "think twice" where the legality of an order is in doubt, granting the superior orders defense unless there is *no* doubt about its unlawful nature. East German law, in contrast, assumes that there is a duty to examine "whether the order, recognizable for everyone, violates criminal and international law."

The BGH found the superior orders defense did not apply to the defendants. The court argued that, despite the high degree of political indoctrination to which the border soldiers had been exposed, even for them "the elementary prohibition to kill was obvious," and that besides "the great majority of the GDR population disapproved of the use of firearms at the border." This result raises the question whether anything is really left to the more lenient nature of the West German law, at least in cases involving the protection of life.

Rejecting the "superior orders" defense did not, however, settle the question of culpability. The possible defense of unavoidable lack of consciousness of wrongdoing, according to which the defendants would have acted "without guilt," remained. Here, too, the courts did not see much difficulty: the LG Berlin held that even the "intellectually simple-minded" defendants, whose personal development had been influenced by a rigid military training, could have realized that military duty does not justify all conduct. If they believed their conduct to be justified, their mistake was not unavoidable since life is the highest of all legal interests. The BGH felt it could not take exception to this view, adding that the trial judge could also have pointed out that in the course of their training the border soldiers had been told they did not have to follow orders requiring them to act inhumanely.

The court only briefly considered GDR criminal law doctrine as possibly more lenient. GDR doctrine apparently would have cast the issue as one of lack of intent, intent requiring that the perpetrator knew that he was violating basic social norms. The difference is important because for the defense of lack of intent it is irrelevant whether the underlying erroneous assumptions were avoidable, making lack of intent a much stronger defense than lack of consciousness of wrongdoing. But the court dismissed the issue because it was not convinced that under GDR law it would have constituted lack of intent to believe that an order must be followed even if it violates the criminal law.

In sum, the BGH deserves criticism not only for failing to scrutinize more closely the nature of the actual orders and the defendant's ability to recognize them as wrong but also for dismissing in such shortcut fashion the possibility that the application of GDR criminal law doctrine might have led to an exoneration of the defendants based on lack of intent.

Special Problems in Prosecuting Top-Level Decision Makers

In the meantime, a number of top-level decision makers have been prosecuted in a trial that became known as the Honecker case. Erich Honecker, the former state council and SED party chairman, and other top-level officials close to him were charged with manslaughter based on selected cases of killings at the inter-German border. Particularly the fact that Honecker himself was to stand trial in unified Germany was spectacular and caused fervent public debate. On the one hand, there was a strong feeling that the "big fish" should not be able to act with impunity while the little fish are caught. On the other, some questioned whether the Unification Treaty provided sufficient basis for the unified German state to assume jurisdiction and punitive power over the representatives of the former East German state, and whether staging a criminal trial against Honecker could really further societal peace. Moreover, the prospect arose that adherence to rule of law and fair trial standards could hamper prosecution of these defendants, who were aged and ailing; allegedly, Honecker was terminally ill with cancer.

Issues of jurisdiction and sovereign immunity had been cleared by the high courts early on, and Honecker's ability to stand trial became the main issue.

After two months of a trial that became largely entangled in medical questions over the nature and severity of Honecker's illness, the proceedings against him had to be dismissed. Berlin's newly established state constitutional court, in one of its first cases, ruled that continued detention would constitute a violation of human dignity. Honecker left for Chile on January 12, 1993; the German people were left divided over the question of whether respecting the rule of law's procedural guarantees in Honecker's case, too, has been a deplorable surrender or a healthy triumph of the Rechsstaat.

The trial continued against former members of the National Defense Council Heinz Keßler, Fritz Streletz, and Heinz Albrecht. Based on their roles in the decision-making process and execution of government policy regarding border violations, the LG Berlin held them responsible for the deaths of seven people who had been killed between 1971 and 1989 in an attempt to flee across the inter German border. According to the criminal law in the former GDR, however, full criminal liability for the indirect commission of a crime was limited to circumstances in which the direct perpetrators were not responsible themselves. Since this was not the case here, the LG convicted these higher-ups only as accessories (instigators) to the crimes of the lower ranks who had actually shot at the fugitives or operated the land mines. The defendants received sentences of imprisonment between seven-and-a-half and four-and-a-half years.

The BGH, on appeal, tightened this judgment. The court reiterated that the GDR state practice at the border constituted an "obvious, unbearable" violation of elementary norms of justice and internationally protected human rights and therefore could not provide grounds of justification for any of the individuals who were responsible for the killings of fugitives, directly or indirectly. The court then examined whether the rear ranks should have been held responsible as principals. Under the law of the Federal Republic this turned on the issue of control: Could these defendants be deemed to have acted "through" others, although those others had all acted themselves with full legal responsibility? Based on standards of factual control, the court answered in the affirmative, thereby settling a longstanding doctrinal controversy over the "principal behind the principal." Rear ranks are responsible as principals where they act within the framework of an organizational structure in which their acts lead to a regular course of events; where they take advantage of such structures, in particular of the unconditional readiness of others to fulfil the elements of crime; and where they "want" the end result "as a result of their own actions." Applying these criteria to the defendants here, the court found that they were perpetrators of manslaughter, based on the fact that they had been members of the National Defense Council on whose decisions the implementation of the border practice rested. Those who actually killed fugitives in execution of this policy acted as subordinates in a military hierarchy and as such were "fixed" in their roles.

The style and language of the court's opinion suggests that a new precedent with potentially far-reaching consequences beyond government criminality is being set. In the context of the killings at the Berlin Wall, it is yet an open question to what extent intermediate officers can be held criminally responsible under this precedent. So far, homicide prosecutions have concentrated on the border soldiers and on the top-level leaders.

Criminal Sanctions

Considering the sentences in the first two *Mauerschützen* proceedings before the LG Berlin, it looks as though the courts have sought to soften the rather rigorously found manslaughter verdicts by means of lenient sentencing. In both proceedings the accusations were reduced from attempted manslaughter to attempted manslaughter in a minor degree. In support, the courts primarily pointed to the fact that the defendants were brought up in a repressive system that through its schools, mass organizations, and "political education" in the military had contributed to the deformation of their Rechtsbewußtsein, or sense of right. This reduction lowered the sentencing range for manslaughter from "not under five years" to "six months to five years" for manslaughter in a minor degree, with an additional reduction for attempt. With the exception of one defendant who was sentenced to a three-and-a-half-year term of imprisonment, the other defendants received sentences between one-and-a-half and two years and were granted probation.

In determining the individual sentences, the courts had to consider the degree of the defendants' culpability. In its appellate opinion, the BGH in its first Mauerschützen case summarily accepted the LG Berlin's reasoning, which had considered in mitigation the fact that the defendants grew up after the Berlin Wall was built and that therefore their personal backgrounds made them unable to assess critically their indoctrination. Furthermore, the court recognized that the defendants were soldiers at the "very bottom" of the military hierarchy and that "in a certain way" were themselves victims of the "circumstances." Finally, the court shared the LG Berlin's desire for leniency because the soldiers were being held criminally responsible at a time when functionaries "who had a greater overview and a more differentiated training" had not been tried or sentenced.

Sentencing in these types of cases is fraught with difficulties. What functions does punishment serve in politically "tainted" human rights cases, and what kinds of sanctions are appropriate? A probationary sentence, for example, is arguably a "system-bound" sanction in that it is primarily designed to resocialize the defendant. From this point of view, the purpose of probation becomes futile to the extent that the society and its norms toward which resocialization was aimed has ceased to exist. The benefit of a sentence of probation is then the avoidance of the negative effects of imprisonment. Probation in this context actually amounts to abstention from execution of punishment. Whereas abstaining from punishment is a sentencing option, albeit very limited, in our present law, mere abstaining from execution of punishment is not.

Yet in many cases it is uncertain whether any of the traditional forms of punishment, especially imprisonment, can serve a legitimate penal purpose for human rights violations that are a product of norms sanctioned by a vanished political system. The justification of punishment of human rights violators based on the theory of deterrence is questionable when a need for deterrence is not discernible. This is especially so where the political system that engaged in human rights violations has been replaced by another system whose institutions are not likely to follow the same example, as in the case of unified Germany. Another, so-called positive general prevention theory seeks to justify criminal sanctions on the basis of the need for symbolic norm affirmation. But on the one hand, the GDR norms need not and should no longer be affirmed, and on the other, the defendants cannot be required retroactively to accept the norms of the Federal Republic. Thus, the theory is plausible only if, on a higher supra political level, punishment can be deemed to affirm the continuing validity of inalienable human rights. If the purpose of punishment is to enforce and reaffirm norms, not to make norms, the normative basis here would have to be an internationally recognized set of rules with regard to the protection of life and the right to leave one's country. As we have seen, however, a firm consensus on this remains elusive. But to the extent that the normative basis is lacking or incomplete, the symbolic powers of punishment are really employed for non formation, not norm-affirmation purposes.

Another problem is that by overemphasizing the abstract norm level, theories of "positive" general prevention run the risk of justifying results disconnected from the concrete harm. In contrast, the harm level is taken into account by theories that seek to balance concerns for both prevention and justice. The need to safeguard societal peace and restore equity is taken into account. Penal sanctioning is based on the individual offender's guilt in violating essential norms and thereby causing harm or danger to both individuals and community and on the need to provide a fair remedy. Such an approach is significantly distinct from notions of "retribution" and "just deserts." Unlike these (purely punitive) theories, this approach allows and seeks an integration (not simply addition) of punitive and restorative remedies; it assumes that a fair remedy need not necessarily be either a "proportional" or a stigmatizing one in order to fulfil the purposes of the criminal law. Such a theory of punishment might also be better suited to addressing "politically tainted" human rights violations, provided that it combines concerns for the victim's rights with further humanization of sanctions for the offender.

In general, we should therefore seek alternatives to

imprisonment where possible. One option is to extend the range of sentences eligible for suspension. While maintaining the symbolic power of imposing a sentence that is adequate to the guilt of the offender, the negative consequences of desocialization through execution of that sentence are avoided. Suspension can be combined with lesser stigmatizing and restorative sanctions for the benefit of the victims, their families, and the community. It seems that these avenues have been ignored in the *Mauerschützen* cases.

Some types of sanctions may be particularly suited to address human rights violations. For instance, as Roht-Arriaza has suggested, the loss of pension rights and other sanctions related to the official function that was abused, directly or indirectly, seem worthy of further consideration. On pension rights, the Unification Treaty in its chapter on *"Employment and Social Order,"* in fact, provides that as a matter of social security law (i.e., not depending on a conviction in criminal court) "unjustified" and "excessive" pension benefits from "special" and "supplemental" insurance systems shall be denied or reduced. The former insurance covers persons serving for the government in a special "service and trust" relationship for instance in the Stasi or the military whereas the latter covers various professional groups, in particular those deemed "intelligentsia." In particular, pension benefits shall be reduced or denied for beneficiaries who violated the "principles of humanity or the rule of law" or gravely abused their positions to their own advantage or to the detriment of others.

Whether such "welfare sanctions" globally imposed on "system-closed" segments of society will withstand judicial scrutiny, including review by the constitutional court, remains to be seen. Among the pivotal questions should be whether and to what extent such sanctions are tantamount to a public judgment of personal, blameworthy wrongdoing and may therefore represent punishment. This would make imposition of such sanctions subject to procedural and substantive constitutional guarantees, especially that of *nulla poena sine culpa*, and require a finding of individual criminal culpability in a fair proceeding respecting the presumption of innocence.

In general, however, suffice it to say that our general criminal sanctions presently focus on the deprivation of physical liberty and financial means and are relatively antipathetic to the deprivation of professional, political, and property rights as forms of punishment. However, not only the recent deliberations at the 1992 meeting of the Deutscher Juristentag, but also the newly introduced forfeiture of property as punishment indicate growing dissatisfaction with the traditional criminal sanctions.

Conclusion: Some Perspectives on Criminal Justice in Human Rights Cases

The *Mauerschützen* cases in unified Germany illustrate that blaming and punishing individuals for human rights violations within the framework of the criminal justice system is fraught with difficulties. First, the traditional principles of criminal responsibility were designed to deal with conduct and the conduct-result relation where individuals act alone or in concert with a few others; they were not intended for larger organizational structures that tend to dilute the individual's personal responsibility for a particular result. Second, Germany's particular historic situation of reunification forecloses direct scrutiny of GDR law and practice by the principles embodied in the constitution of the Federal Republic. Forced to rely on international law, we have to realize that there are considerable gray areas concerning the recognition of, commitment to, and national enforcement of important human rights that ought to be beyond the reach of national governments. Third, not only unified Germany but successor governments in general, willing to prosecute criminal human rights violations that occurred under a former regime, will face problems regarding the prohibition of *ex post facto* punishment entrenched in the rule of law. Fourth, another major problem arising in the area of criminal human rights violations relates to the question of appropriate sanctions.

At present, academic discussion in Germany is largely concerned with the problem of ex post facto punishment. The BGH in the *Mauerschützen* case found a way out without fully addressing the problem, by framing the decisive issue as one of "right interpretation" of the GDR border law at the time of conduct. Yet it would be more straightforward to assume that criminal prosecution conflicted directly with the *ex post facto* prohibition, and to ask whether its protection is subject to inherent limitations. Such a limiting approach could build on the idea that the individual's reliance deserves strongest protection where ex ante definition of criminal conduct is at issue but potentially less protection regarding the reliance on exemptions from punishment. Arguments in support could rely on both natural law and international law, in that there appears to be an emerging obligation under customary international law to investigate grave human rights violations and take action against those responsible. Arguably, such an obligation, including the obligation to provide redress to victims, is incorporated into German constitutional law; the German Grundgesetz in article 1, clause 2 professes the German people's respect for "inviolable and inalienable human rights as the basis of all human community, peace and justice in the world." Under this approach, not all crimes committed by an oppressive government can justify overriding the ex post facto prohibition, but only cases of sufficient gravity. Undoubtedly, this would be the case where the violation amounts to an international crime namely, a crime against humanity. Below this level, sufficient gravity exists where human rights are being violated in reliance on laws, regulations, orders, or state practice that were recognizably meant to exempt such violations from being subject to punishment, or where the interpretation and application of the law amounts to an obvious, grave human rights violation.

And yet, considering the numerous problems in blaming and punishing individuals for human rights violations, are there really viable alternatives to criminal prosecution? The idea of amnesty has not found support in Germany; in particular, it is argued that there is no basis for amnesty before the allocation of criminal responsibility. To be sure, only many years down the line will the extent of *de facto* amnesties (amnesties resulting from non prosecution) be verifiable. In addition, the idea of a "national tribunal" and other forms of community catharsis that have been advanced by voices from the former GDR seem to have lost their initial appeal.

Considering the hundreds of norms that criminal laws do protect by the threat of punishment, it seems paradoxical that some of the gravest violations leave modern societies more or less perplexed. The prosecution of "little fish" raises serious quandaries because the definition of what is right or wrong as a matter of law has traditionally been within the domain of national sovereignty and national policies. The protection of universal human rights, therefore, will always be subject to compromise so long as the sovereigns cannot be forced to observe these rights in making national law. The considerable doubts and gray areas concerning the international status of the right to the protection of life, as evidenced, for instance, in the use of deadly force against border violators, must be clarified.

Adjudicating the criminal responsibility of "big fish," particularly leading state representatives, for grave human rights violations requires considering an international solution. The legitimacy of holding individuals responsible in a criminal court would then be based on international legal consensus that no nation could disregard without justifying itself on the basis of specific, internationally recognized grounds. Nations would not, as is the case in Germany today, be suspected of engaging in political self-righteousness or even *Siegerjustiz* (victor's justice) and "political trials"; instead, the state could assume the role of complaining party which seems a more fitting role than that of judge with respect to the offensive state practices in question. Thus, the example of the Honecker case provides additional impetus to proceed with the long-deliberated establishment of an international criminal court. In the course of working out further details, the question of sanctions should merit special attention, a topic that opens new and challenging fields for academics as well as practitioners.

9

Negotiating Changes for Human Rights in South Africa

Introduction

The political situation then remained relatively calm until the 1976 Soweto uprisings, occasioned by the police shooting of African schoolchildren who were peacefully protesting the use of Afrikaans in the schools. Months of unrest followed throughout the country, during which time the government augmented its arsenal of security legislation and eventually achieved relative quiet. It was, however, the proverbial calm before the storm.

Protest began anew with the formation of a broad-based umbrella organization of anti-apartheid groups known as the United Democratic Front (UDF). With the emergence of the UDF, anti-government protests reached unprecedented heights. So great was the perceived threat to the government that then-President P. W. Botha elevated the security forces to a new level of authority within the government. From the mid-1980s, the country was ruled under a nationwide state of emergency accompanied by especially stringent security legislation. Troops were omnipresent in the black townships, and thousands of people, including children as young as eight years, were detained without trial. Allegations of torture were widespread. At the same time, the rise of vigilantism in the townships and a series of assassinations of prominent anti-apartheid activists led to suspicion that the government or its agents were conducting an extralegal campaign of terror. As the decade came to a close, Botha, who had suffered a stroke, was replaced by F. W. de Klerk. De Klerk, in a series of moves that startled both South Africans and foreign observers, set South Africa on the road toward a negotiated settlement of the political crisis.

Almost from the start, the question of the treatment of those both within the government and within the opposition who had committed human rights abuses became a contentious issue. The identification and punishment of persons responsible for extralegal killings and massacres, the fate of political prisoners, and the role of an amnesty all continue to be major points of discussion and discord. As South Africa moved toward and beyond its first election based on universal suffrage, it faced hard questions of how, and to what extent, to deal with the past.

Negotiations and the Move toward a New Order

On February 2, 1990, President de Klerk announced the lifting of the ban on the ANC, the Pan-Africanist Congress (PAC), the South African Communist Party (SACP), and other groups; the removal of restrictions on thirty-three other organizations, including the powerful Congress of South African Trade Unions; the release of most political prisoners; the repeal of restrictions on 374 freed detainees; the limiting of detention without trial to six months, with provision for legal representation and medical treatment; and a moratorium on hangings. De Klerk also indicated that he would free ANC leader Nelson Mandela, perhaps the world's most famous political prisoner, after twenty-seven years in jail. Thus began the process of political transformation of South Africa.

Mandela's release a few days later was accompanied by jubilation on the part of many of his compatriots as millions of people the world over watched the events on television. Mandela proceeded to tour numerous foreign countries, where he was greeted by adoring crowds. At home, the ANC opened offices throughout the country, and other political groups began to organize their newly legalized operations. In addition, the ANC held meetings with the government on "talks about talks." These discussions yielded the Groote Schuur Minute of May 4, 1990 and the Pretoria Minute of August 6, 1990; the documents established procedures for the release of political prisoners and for the granting of an official indemnity to political exiles. It was envisaged that all political prisoners would be released by April 1991. In fact, the established procedure proved unwieldy, so that by August 1992, the ANC insisted that 400 political prisoners remained incarcerated, a charge the government denied.

Meanwhile, in June, de Klerk announced the lifting of the four-year-old state of emergency. Shortly thereafter, the ANC abandoned the armed struggle, although it did not disband its military wing Unkhonto we Sizwe (Spear of the Nation), a condition the government continued to insist upon.

Many people came to believe de Klerk's promise in his February speech that "henceforth, everybody's political points of view will be tested against their realism, their workability and their fairness. The time for negotiation has arrived." Graffiti in some African townships even proclaimed, "Viva Comrade de Klerk!" Yet euphoria quickly evaporated as people recognized that despite the unprecedented occurrences, the main pieces of apartheid legislation the Land Acts of 1913 and 1936, the Group Areas Act, and the Population Registration Act remained intact. By year's end, South Africa teetered perilously on the brink of collapsing in internecine convulsions as Africans, allegedly with security force or other government complicity, brutalized and murdered one another in areas throughout the country in conflicts fuelled by urban-rural, class, and ethnic tensions.

The February, 1991 opening of Parliament brought further changes. De Klerk announced his intention to remove the pillars of apartheid. However, because blacks lacked the vote, the rescission of the legislation did not alter the balance of power in South Africa. The NP remained firmly in control of the country, commanding the allegiance of the largest and most sophisticated military machine in Africa.

In September, some people saw grounds for cautious optimism when representatives of the government, the ANC, and Inkatha became the major signatories to the National Peace Accord. Thereafter, the NP, in an effort to lead any negotiations in a way that would produce a settlement favourable to its interests, agreed to sit down at the bargaining table with the ANC and members of all political parties that wished to participate. The forum, which became known as the Convention for a Democratic South Africa (CODESA), included representatives from eighteen political parties. Analysis reveals that the perception Pretoria sought to create that CODESA was a vigorous multiparty free-for-all was but an illusion. With the exception of the ANC, Inkatha, and the NP itself, all parties to the left and right with the potential to disrupt the democratization process or undermine a new democratic order chose to absent themselves. With one exception, the other fourteen parties, including the Coloured and Indian parties and those from the African homelands, ' were essentially NP puppets, which owed their existence to Pretoria's largesse and had negligible support from the populace.

On December 20, 1991, sixteen of the eighteen parties signed the Declaration of Intent. The Declaration provided that CODESA would "set in motion the process of drawing up and establishing a constitution" guaranteeing that South Africa would be "a united, democratic, nonracial and nonsexist state," with a constitution as the supreme law and "an independent, nonracial and impartial judiciary" to interpret that constitution. In addition, the parties subscribed to the ideas that South Africa would be a multiparty democracy with universal adult suffrage, a common voters' roll, and a basic electoral system based on proportional representation. The parties also agreed upon "a separation of powers between the legislature, executive and judiciary with appropriate checks and balances." "The diversity of languages, cultures and religions of the people of South Africa" also was to be recognized. All were to enjoy "human rights, freedoms and civil liberties protected by an entrenched and justiciable Bill of Rights and a legal system that guarantees equality of all before the law."

De Klerk at first indicated that an interim government might be quickly established, but almost immediately retreated from that position. On March 17, 1992, in an effort to show that he had broad support for his initiatives, de Klerk staged a referendum among white voters. They were asked to respond yes or no to the question, "Do you support the continuation of the reform process which the State President began on February 2, 1990 and which is aimed at a new constitution through negotiation?" With an 87.6 percent voter turnout, 68.7 percent voted in favour of de Klerk's policies. The white voters did so perhaps out of fear that a "no" vote would plunge the country into civil war and in spite of a vigorous campaign by the official parliamentary opposition Conservative Party. De Klerk's ostensible victory cleared the way for negotiations to proceed apace. However, further talks deadlocked over the power of the executive until an interim government could be formed, the fate of the remaining political prisoners, and the percentage of votes required for decisions by the proposed interim assembly with regard to regional borders, government powers, and various regional issues.

Violence and the Goldstone Commission

The NP, ANC, and Inkatha (now formally known as the Inkatha Freedom Party, or IFP) continued to express their desire for talks about change. However, they did so against a backdrop of increasing violence in the black community. Indeed, from July 1990 through June 1992, some 6,229 South Africans died in violent incidents, approximately the same number killed during the unrest of the 1980s. The ANC alleged that the deteriorating conditions were not merely the result of black animosities but rather were being orchestrated by a "third force" operating either under government auspices or with government approval.

After considerable public outcry, de Klerk appointed a commission of inquiry, known officially as the Commission of Inquiry into Public Violence and Intimidation. The Commission quickly became known as the Goldstone Commission, after the judge who presided over the Appellate Division, South Africa's highest court. The Commission's mandate included investigating certain particularly notorious massacres and other acts of violence and attempting to discover the extent of involvement by security forces or forces under the control of the ANC, Inkatha, PAC, or other groups. Despite its official mandate, the Commission initially had few resources and no investigative capacity of its own, but relied instead on reports by the police or independent human rights groups. The Commission had no mandate in the nominally independent black homelands; nor did the government have to act on the evidence of misconduct it produced. It carried out over forty investigations and won a reputation for evenhandedness.

The Goldstone Commission was called upon regularly to investigate incidents of violence that threatened to derail the negotiation process. In May 1992, the Commission issued a report on the causes of violence, placing primary blame on the ANC and Inkatha and finding no evidence of government complicity. A month later, on June 17, forty-five ANC supporters were killed in Boipatong township south of Johannesburg by Inkatha Freedom Party members who lived in a hostel for migrant workers. The ANC pulled out of negotiations, accusing government security forces of abetting the perpetrators. De Klerk denied such suggestions and asked that the Goldstone Commission add the Boipatong, massacre to its investigative agenda.

Over a year later, the Commission found no conclusive evidence that the South African Defence Force had trained Inkatha supporters to perpetrate violence. After considerable jockeying and in the midst of escalating violence, the government and the ANC agreed to meet in a two-day "bush summit" at the end of October. By then, commentators were arguing that the ANC favoured bilateral over multiparty negotiations and that the government was interested in a power sharing arrangement with the ANC. The planned summit stalled for months on the issues of power sharing and a decentralized federal government.

United Nations Becomes Involved

The impasse over further negotiations led the ANC to propose international involvement in halting the violence and accelerating the transition to majority rule. Speaking at a U.N. Security Council emergency meeting over the Boipatong massacre, Mandela called for a permanent U.N. presence in the country in the form of a special envoy who would investigate the causes of the violence and "provide the council with information for further measures to end the violence, including continuous monitoring of the situation." In response, the United Nations sent former U.S. Secretary of State Cyrus Vance as a special envoy on a ten-day mission aimed at getting the government and the ANC to resume their talks.

One outcome of the U.N. visit was the stationing of international observers to monitor the violence. Secretary-General Boutros Boutros-Ghali, favouring a return to the bargaining table, proposed in a report to the Security Council that thirty U.N. observers be stationed in South Africa to bolster the National Peace Accord; by September, fifty observers had arrived. By that time the international community was becoming increasingly involved in efforts to stop the violence in South Africa and ensure a smooth transition to democracy. In addition to the U.N. monitors, teams from the World Council of Churches, the European Community, the Commonwealth, and the Organization of African Unity were either beginning operations or planning to begin them in the near future. In addition to a National Peace Secretariat composed of representatives of the political parties, the Goldstone Commission helped coordinate the observers and used them to buttress the commission's fact-finding abilities.

In addition, the secretary-general's report of August 7 commended the Goldstone Commission's work and called on it to investigate the behaviour of not only the government-controlled security forces but also various private security agencies, the military wings of the ANC and PAC, and the Buthelezi-controlled police force of the KwaZulu homeland. The report also called upon the government to give the Commission greater powers of investigation into the causes of violence and asked for international assistance for its operation. Finally, the secretary-general recommended an amnesty for all political offenders.

Question of Amnesty

The Commission responded positively to the U.N. suggestions and asked for a general amnesty so that its work could be made "more efficient." In other remarks, Justice Goldstone suggested that some form of amnesty would be needed to encourage people with inside knowledge of violent events to come forward. Shortly thereafter, the government and the ANC were reported to be discussing a general amnesty plan put forward by the United Nations aimed at restarting the move toward an interim government. Under the plan members of the security forces who had been involved in actions against the ANC as well as anti-apartheid activists were to receive blanket immunity; the 420 captives the ANC insisted were political prisoners were also to be freed.

From the beginning, the NP government had tried to tie the question of an amnesty for its own forces to the freeing of the remaining prisoners. One early stumbling block was the government's steadfast refusal to release prisoners sentenced for offenses such as murder, terrorism, and arson on behalf of political organizations. In November 1991, the government issued Guidelines for Defining Political Offenses, which extended the definition of a political prisoner to include those who had advanced apartheid policies. Now, ostensibly viewing the idea as a way to build on its own earlier Guidelines and to protect its agents, the NP government immediately seized upon the U.N. suggestion and proposed that the ANC accept such a policy in exchange for the release of the political prisoners.

The ANC rejected the suggestion of a blanket amnesty. On August 13, an ANC press release emphasized that the discussion of amnesty should be reserved for "an interim government of National Unity" and that such an amnesty could be granted only if the people agreed. In addition, the document pointed out that an amnesty would not further the Goldstone Commission's investigations because the courts already had the authority to grant individuals immunity from prosecution. Furthermore, both the ANC and Bishop Desmond Tutu indicated that any amnesty would have to be accompanied by full disclosure of the past activities of the security forces, including their complicity in factional violence in the townships. An ANC spokesperson added that the ANC might be more willing to consider an amnesty for older crimes, but certainly not for those committed while the negotiations were under way. Finally, the ANC refused to let the problem of the political prisoners be tied to the amnesty question and suspended all discussion of both subjects.

Shortly thereafter, de Klerk, who clung to his long-held position that he knew of no one in the government engaged in nefarious activities, on October 16 introduced into Parliament an amnesty bill just as testimony began before the Goldstone Commission's inquiry into alleged police involvement and Complicity. The bill, which gave the president sweeping powers of indemnity, was debated in committee on October 18. It immediately became a contentious issue; debate required postponing the conclusion of a special session of Parliament when it appeared the bill was going down to defeat.

On October 19, de Klerk publicly expressed his support for the measure at the Transvaal Law Society's centenary celebration. De Klerk said the bill's purpose was to "level the playing field" between the government and its opponents. He insisted that as head of the government I do not know of any single individual by name employed by the state in the police, in the defence force, or in any other capacity, who committed any crime. I don't have a list, I don't have any plans to take any initiative to submit any names to the board which is to be established in terms of the legislation. No doubt, there might be such individuals. I don't know who they are. If we knew who they were we would have charged them with the crimes they committed. I would like to stress that this legislation is not aimed at clearing the decks for intransigent government which participated behind the scenes in all sorts of criminal activities.

Still, despite this public plea, the bill failed to receive the necessary majorities in the segregated tricameral Parliament. The bill passed handily in the NP-dominated white House of Assembly over the objections of the Democratic Party, which insisted that there be public disclosure of the behaviour of those indemnified. It also passed readily in the Coloured House of Representatives, despite criticism from the minority Labour Party. However, Solidarity, the majority party in the Indian House of Delegates was steadfast in its refusal to ratify the bill. The discussion over amnesty was further complicated when the Goldstone Commission revealed that top military officers had been involved in a campaign to discredit the ANC.

Consequently, de Klerk overcame his rebuff by resorting to the president's council, the parliamentary body that resolved legislative disputes among the three houses. The council was dominated by the National Party, which had thirty-five votes in the sixty-member body, a 58 percent majority. The council had last been called upon by P. W. Botha, de Klerk's predecessor, in 1986 when he used it to enact security legislation opposed by the Labour Party. In 1989, the council itself suggested that it be restructured. By using this route, on November 9, de Klerk enacted the Further Indemnity Act.

The act provided the state president with the authority to grant amnesty to those who "advised, directed, commanded, ordered or performed any act with a political object." Although the act applied to acts committed before October 8, 1990, a discretionary clause gave the state president the power to enlarge the period as he deemed appropriate, and there was some indication that the government intended to amend the law to extend to late 1992. Persons seeking amnesty applied individually to a National Council on Indemnity, which heard their case in secret. Not only Council members but also those present at the proceedings were to take an oath of secrecy. Any contravention of the secrecy provision was a crime punishable by a fine or a one-year prison term. Although the names of those granted indemnity would be published, their offenses and the identities of their victims would not be disclosed. Those granted indemnity would no longer be subject to either criminal prosecution or civil suits. Because it required individual presentation to the council on indemnity, government spokespersons argued the bill did not constitute a blanket amnesty but merely a "procedural mechanism."

The ANC, of course, vociferously opposed the legislation, which it considered an effort by the government to pardon police, military, and security force members implicated in the commission of heinous acts. It was adamant that criminals could not pardon themselves and indicated that it would not abide by the legislation if it came to power. Nonetheless, on November 18, the ANC formally adopted a discussion document, entitled Strategic Perspectives, which supported a possible power-sharing arrangement with the Np. The document recognized the desirability of a general amnesty for security force and civil service members because such individuals have the power to obstruct the transition.

Before leaving office, de Klerk commuted the sentences of almost 100 convicted prisoners and granted amnesty to several former security officials, thus attempting to remove any chance that information on their activities would become public. These indemnities and sentence reductions were frozen and referred to President Mandela for judgment.

The ANC's Own Abuses

The ANC also worked to bolster opposition to the amnesty bill by the carefully timed release of a report conducted by an ANC commission of inquiry into atrocities committed in ANC refugee camps in Zambia, Angola, Tanzania, and Uganda. The Commission, which was composed of three lawyers one independent and two ANC members had been appointed in March 1992 after former refugees repeatedly alleged that torture and other forms of mistreatment were widespread. The commission completed its report in August.

The findings, which Mandela announced at a news conference, recognized that the acts committed included torture, which contravened both the ANC's code of conduct and former ANC President Oliver Tambo's 1980 pledge to honour the Geneva Conventions. The Commission warned that the ANC would suffer from continued accusations, malaise, and recriminations unless the organization expanded the investigation. Thus, it recommended that the ANC "cleanse" itself of persons who had committed atrocities and urged that the guilty be barred from positions of authority.

Recognizing that its own membership was weighted in favour of the ANC, the commission urged that a more independent commission of inquiry be formed to explore allegations of disappearance and murder of which it had become aware and bring those responsible to justice. Furthermore, the commission urged that victims receive compensation for their treatment as well as psychological, medical, and educational assistance. Acknowledging these recommendations, at his press conference Mandela stated that "as a leadership we accept ultimate responsibility for not adequately monitoring and therefore eradicating such abuses." He pledged that the ANC would immediately examine the recommendations and act appropriately. The obvious intent was to contrast the ANC's handling of humanitarian law violations and abuses within its own ranks with the government's attempted blanket amnesty.

As 1993 began, the amnesty issue, and that of the ANC's conduct, continued to draw attention. The right-wing International Freedom Foundation had appointed a commission led by a British barrister named R. S. Douglas to investigate the behaviour of the ANC in its camps for political exiles. In mid-January, the Douglas Commission issued a report condemning ANC behaviour as a gross violation of human rights. The ANC's response was not to deny the charges which it could not do in light of its own earlier revelations about atrocities but to minimize the severity of what had occurred. The controversy deepened when the conservative Europe-based International Society for Human Rights endorsed the Douglas Commission Report and argued that "if the ANC were a government, then the U.N. would have already appointed a special human rights rapporteur to investigate." Also in this vein, the *Sunday Tunes*, not known for its radical views, in an editorial castigated the behaviour of both the government and the ANC and called for an accounting to the international community.

This attempt to exonerate the "security establishment" of the ANC, and to cover up its crimes, bears striking resemblance to the government's attempts to exonerate its own security establishment and to cover up its own crimes the guilty all the guilty must be brought to justice if necessary, by the international community.

The ANC followed up in January 1993 by appointing a commission to examine allegations of human rights abuses in its detention centers in exile. The commission was led by a black South African businessman who was assisted by a Zimbabwean judge and an American lawyer. The commission's August 1993 report found that at least two senior ANC officials had violated the rights of detainees. These were Joe Modise, commander of the ANC's military wing and a central figure in negotiations over the structure of the new national defense force, and Jacob Zuma, former ANC intelligence chief and executive committee member who was thought by observers of South African politics to be a likely candidate for a major role in a reconstructed police force. The commission also found that several security officials, including three members of the ANC's security department, were involved in violations, including torture, execution, arbitrary detention, and various types of inhuman treatment. Although the ANC's code of conduct provided a maximum penalty of suspension or expulsion from the organization, the commission went much further in its recommendations. It suggested that the ANC apologize and give compensation to victims of abuse. To this end, it recommended the ANC create a claims settlement agency to give awards to persons who suffered abuse as well as to the families of those who perished. The Commission also recommended that the organization keep relatives of those missing in the camps informed of continuing investigations. Finally, those former detainees who wished to rejoin the ANC should be permitted to do so. Commenting on the report, Mandela, reflecting the views of many ANC members who were never in exile and who have favoured disclosure of wrongdoing, said that the ANC was taking the commission's recommendations "very seriously. We have taken the first important step of taking the public into our confidence as to what the commission has recommended." The report was heralded by the diplomatic and academic communities as an important act of self-criticism not typical of South African political organizations. In contrast, the NP was quick to try to capitalize on the findings for political advantage. It claimed that the report revealed the ANC could not run the country by itself. The NP also challenged the ANC to have persons accused of abuses submit to the legal process. However, the NP's call for ANC action made no suggestion that a similar course of behaviour be followed by the NP with regard to its agents.

Outcome of the Negotiations

On November 26, 1993, de Klerk announced that he wanted a fully representative government of national unity in place no later than the first half of 1994. In response, the ANC criticized de Klerk for anticipating the outcome of the pending bilateral talks and for refusing to accede to its prior demand for elections before the end of 1993. Days later, Buthelezi announced that he had plans for a new constitution in Natal province, an area including the KwaZulu homeland, which would result in an autonomous state. The danger of secession orchestrated by Buthelezi was bad enough; shortly thereafter the Azanian People's Liberation Army (APLA), the military wing of the Pan-Africanist Congress (PAC), in a series of attacks on a golf club and a steakhouse, declared war on all white South Africans. The government then broke off all talks with the PAC.

In the midst of this instability, the chance of insurrection by elements within the military and a campaign of right-wing terror was exacerbated by a December 19 announcement by de Klerk. In contrast to his prior defense of the security forces, de Klerk dismissed or suspended twenty-three military officers, including six generals who were suspected of activities, including assassination, aimed at thwarting racial reconciliation. While de Klerk's actions could be construed as a major concession to the ANC, which had urged a purge of the military as a condition for the resumption of multiparty discussions, there was the danger that his actions would push increasing numbers of whites into the arms of the Conservative Party and extra parliamentary groups to its right.

In mid-August, as negotiations continued, widespread suspicion about government efforts to cover-up past misdeeds was bolstered by revelations that the state security council had instructed government departments to destroy classified documents.

Although the question of dealing with human rights violators remained unresolved, in October, as the prospect loomed large of concluding the multiparty negotiations with a new constitutional arrangement, de Klerk and Mandela shared the Nobel Peace Prize for their work toward effecting a peaceful transition in their country. Shortly thereafter, on November 18, de Klerk, Mandela, and the leaders of eighteen of the nineteen other parties remaining in the negotiations endorsed a new constitution that combines provisions for majority rule with those safeguarding minority rights. Inkatha and a number of right-wing Afrikaner groups refused to endorse the agreement, seeking greater autonomy. The 142-page constitution is to remain in effect until the Parliament a 400-seat assembly and a 90seat senate, which chooses the president elected April 27, 1994, drafts a permanent one, a process estimated to take two years. The constitution provides for minority seats in a twenty-seven member cabinet for five years; safeguards the positions and pensions of white civil servants and military personnel; divides the country into nine provinces the four currently existing provinces and the homelands that were abolished with considerable power over their police, educational system, hospitals, and other public services. The constitution also contains a long list of fundamental rights, including a prohibition of torture and three pages of limitations on the president's power to declare a state of emergency. An eleven member constitutional court, whose members are appointed by the President from a list drawn up by an independent commission, is to construe these rights. The interim constitution's final paragraphs deal with the issue of reconciliation and amnesty:

The pursuit of national unity, the well-being of all South African citizens and peace require reconciliation between the people of South Africa and the reconstruction of society. The adoption of this Constitution lays the secure foundation for the people of South Africa to transcend the divisions and strife of the past, which generated gross violations of human rights, the transgression of humanitarian principles in violent conflicts and a legacy of hatred, fear, guilt and revenge. These can now be addressed on the basis that there is a need for understanding but not for vengeance, a need for reparation but not for retaliation. In order to advance such reconciliation and reconstruction amnesty shall be granted in respect of acts, omissions and offenses associated with political objectives and committed in the course of the conflicts of the past. To this end Parliament shall adopt a law determining a firm cut-off date, which shall be a date after 8 October, 1990 and before 6 December, 1993, and providing for the mechanisms, criteria and procedures, including tribunals, if any, through which such amnesty should be dealt with at any time after the law has been passed.

The April 1994 parliamentary elections, the inauguration of Nelson Mandela as President of South Africa, and his appointment of de Klerk and Buthelezi as members of an ANC-dominated cabinet of national unity ushered in a new epoch in South African politics. The elections themselves were described by one government official as "unmitigated chaos" and were boycotted by most of the white right-wing groups. A spate of bombings in the two days proceeding the elections resulted in the arrest of thirty-five white rightists.

The new government was welcomed internationally. On June 23, 1994, South Africa reclaimed its seat at the

United Nations General Assembly. The Security Council terminated the mandate of the United Nations Observer Mission in South Africa five days later.

Mandela Government's Proposed Measures to Deal with Past Violators

The question of how to treat human rights violators from the days of NP rule on the side of the government and abuses on the side of its foes has come to occupy considerable space in the political landscape. President de Klerk's hurried passage of the Further Indemnity Act over the objections of his own Parliament did not display a willingness on his part to subject persons suspected of nefarious activities to standards of international law. The act had three especially glaring shortcomings. First, the aura of secrecy that surrounded the entire process created the impression that the government would use the process to name only a few token perpetrators while concealing the extent of government-sanctioned or officially orchestrated abuses of human rights of the type revealed in forums such as the Goldstone Commission hearings. Second, the provision forbidding criminal penalties evinced the government's unwillingness to bring the guilty to justice. Third, the language barring civil suits indicated a lack of empathy for victims and their families, who may have been irreparably harmed physically, psychologically, financially, or otherwise by their experience. Thus, the passage of the legislation, rather than becoming a symbol of the government's desire for reconciliation, may have heightened suspicions in the black community that the former government took the behaviour of its agents lightly and has little interest in witnessing the creation of a legal system marked by equality for all under the law.

In contradistinction to the NP government's position, the ANC's posture on the issue of prosecutions is seemingly accepting of international legal standards, its reaction to the Douglas Commission Report notwithstanding. In late 1992, the organization maintained that it is not a question of victors punishing the vanquished, or of anyone losing or saving face, but of joint responsibility undertaken by all South Africans to affirm norms and standards of accountability that become part and parcel of the new democratic society and bind all future governments. People in positions of power, now and in the future, must know that they will be held accountable for abuses of the law and violations of human rights no only by history but by the agencies of law."

The ANC's commitment to this view seems to have been affirmed by its behaviour with regard to the most recent report on abuses. Thus, one of the new government's acts was to announce the formation of a Commission of Truth and Reconciliation. The mandate and proposed working methods of the Commission reflect the South Africans' study of the experience of other countries as well as the advantage of a negotiated transition period in which to think through appropriate guidelines.

As of September 1994, the new government announced that the Truth Commission will establish, in line with international law and the constitution, "as complete a picture as possible of gross human rights violations relating to the conflicts of the past" in and outside South Africa. It will cover events from March 1, 1960, through December 6, 1993; thus, those involved in bombings or other terrorist acts in the pre-electoral period are excluded. It is to prepare a report on such violations and to recommend legal and administrative measures to ensure respect for, and observance of, human rights. The Commission is to be made up of eight to ten members appointed by the president. It will have one year to complete its job, with the option of a six month extension.

One of the commission's most interesting and innovative features is its treatment of the issues of amnesty and prosecution. Those members of political organizations, liberation movements, law enforcement agencies, and security forces who were involved in political crimes may apply to the commission for amnesty and indemnity. However, the commission will only recommend amnesty or indemnity on the basis of full disclosure of the applicant's involvement in the crime, and where the action claimed had a political motive that was capable of being realized. Moreover, the commission's recommendations will not be binding on President Mandela, who will make the final decision as to when amnesty shall apply to a specific individual. As of September 1994, it was unclear the extent to which the commission's proceedings would be public: whereas human rights groups were pushing for open hearings, the National Party and some ANC members preferred secrecy. It is also unclear whether those persons implicated by the testimony of others will be notified and invited to present their own evidence before the commission, and if doing so will automatically constitute an application for amnesty.

The scheme provides a strong incentive for individuals to come forward and seek amnesty. If implicated parties do not come forward by the cut-off date for applications for amnesty, their names may be forwarded to the attorney general to consider prosecution. Thus, rather than a blanket amnesty, the commission's mandate seems to incorporate a massive plea-bargaining arrangement. To receive amnesty, perpetrators may not only have to accept their own responsibility for political crimes but provide any information they may have on the fate of victims or on those higher-ups involved in giving illegal orders. Any prosecutions will take place using existing laws and courts. Nonetheless, where the commission has reasonable grounds to believe there is a risk evidence will be destroyed or tampered with, it may enter premises to search for and seize evidence. These search and seizure provisions are likely to be among the first legal challenges brought under the new Bill of Rights.

The commission's work also evinces a primary concern with victims. Among the commission's objectives is to gather information to make it possible to identify victims and determine their fate or whereabouts, as well as to provide victims with a platform on which they can "express their plight and tell their story." It is to recommend reparations, which may take the form of financial payments or education grants. Indeed, Mandela stressed in a speech marking his first 100 days in office that the "challenge is to ensure that amnesty helps to heal the wounds of the past by also addressing the plight of the victims."

Of course, one of the major challenges confronting the commission will be to design reparations measures that are feasible in light of the enormous economic and social needs of the majority of South Africans and the government's budgetary restraints. An emphasis on government services or grants rather than monetary compensation is likely. Moreover, the commission will face the delicate problem of deciding whether to pass on for possible prosecution the names of high-ranking members of the army or government who are now partners in national unity if they do not come forward voluntarily. The same is true of those members of the ANC responsible for political crimes, and for members of Inkatha. A declared intent to prosecute Inkatha members for the pre-electoral violence if they do not seek amnesty, for example, could unravel an already fragile peace.

The creation of the Truth Commission is, of course, only one part of the larger process of dismantling the apartheid state and creating a new one in its place. The former Guerrilla forces of the ANC are being integrated into the South African National Defence Force, and old officers are being retired. More broadly, apartheid infected every aspect of South African life, from urban design to land tenure to the educational and health systems. The extent to which South Africa can afford to or can afford not to make reparation for these broader injustices is one of the central issues facing the Mandela government.

Nonetheless, the outline of the Truth Commission, including the government's rejection of a blanket amnesty and declared intent to abide by international law on the subject, provides hope that South Africa can provide a successful model of dealing with the past. It remains to be seen whether the operation of the commission bears out that hope.

Bibliography

Agosín, Marjorie, ed. *Women, Gender, and Human Rights: A Global Perspective.* New Brunswick, NJ: Rutgers University Press, 2001.

Baderin, Mashood A. *International Human Rights and Islamic Law.* New York: Oxford University Press, 2003.

Campbell, Tom, Jeffrey Goldsworthy, and Adrienne Stone, eds. *Protecting Human Rights: Instruments and Institutions.* New York: Oxford University Press, 2003.

Dalacoura, Katerina. *Islam, Liberalism and Human Rights.* London: I.B. Tauris, revised ed., 2003.

Emberland, Marius. *The Human Rights of Companies: Exploring the Structure of ECHR Protection.* New York: Oxford University Press, 2006.

Falk, Richard A. *Human Rights Horizons: The Pursuit of Justice in a Globalizing World.* New York: Routledge, 2000.

Goldewijk, B. Klein, A. Contreras Baspineiro and P. Cesar Carbonari. *Dignity and Human Rights: The Implementation of Economic, Social and Cultural Rights.* Ardsley, NY: Transnational

Harris, David and Stephen Livingstone, eds. *The Inter-American System of Human Rights.* NewYork: Oxford University Press, 1998.

Ife, Jim. *Human Rights and Social Work: Towards Rights-Based Practice.* Cambridge, UK: Cambridge University Press, 2001.

Janis, Mark, Richard Kay, and Anthony Bradley. *European Human Rights Law: Texts and Materials.* New York: Oxford University Press, 2nd ed., 2001.

Keal, Paul. *European Conquest and the Rights of Indigenous Peoples: The Moral Backwardness of International Society.* Cambridge, UK: Cambridge University Press, 2003.

Langlois, Anthony J. *The Politics of Justice and Human Rights: Southeast Asia and Universalist Theory.* Cambridge, UK: Cambridge University Press, 2001.

Mahoney, Jack. *The Challenge of Human Rights: Origin, Development, and Significance.* Malden, MA: Blackwell, 2007.

Neyroud, Peter and Alan Beckley. *Policing, Ethics and Human Rights.* Portland, OR: Willan Publ., 2001.

Orend, Brian. *Human Rights: Concept and Context.* Orchard Park, NY: Broadview Press, 2002.

Pasqualucci, Jo M. *The Practice and Procedure of the Inter-American Court of Human Rights.* Cambridge, UK: Cambridge University Press, 2003.

Ratner, Steven R. and Jason S. Abrams. *Accountability for Human Rights Atrocities in International Law: Beyond the Nuremberg Legacy.* New York: Oxford University Press, 2nd ed., 2001.

Salman, Salman M.A. and Siobahn McInerney-Lankford. *The Human Right to Water: Legal and Policy Dimensions.* Washington, DC: The International Bank for Reconstruction and Development/The World Bank, 2004.

Talbott, William J. *Which Rights Should Be Universal?* New York: Oxford University Press, 2005.

Umozurike, Oji. *The African Charter on Human and Peoples' Rights.* The Hague: Nijhoff, 1997.

van der Vyver, Johan D. and John Witte, Jr. *Religious Human Rights in Global Perspective: Legal Perspectives*. The Hague: Kluwer Law International, 1996.

Wellman, Carl. *The Proliferation of Rights: Moral Progress or Empty Rhetoric?* Boulder, CO: Westview Press, 1998.

Zeleza, Paul Tiyambe and Philip J. McConnaughay, eds. *Human Rights, the Rule of Law, and Development in Africa*. Philadelphia, PA: University of Pennsylvania Press, 2004.

Index